Fingerstyle Duets for Ukulele

by Mark Kailana Nelson

Online Audio www.melbay.com/30480BCDEB

Audio Contents

1	Sicilian Waltz	10	'Akaka Falls
2	Simple Gifts	11	Hard Times, Come Again No More
3	The Banks of the Ohio	12	Fandanguillo
4	Margaret's Waltz	13	Home Sweet Home
5	Ahi Wela	14	Sweet Lei Lehua
6	The Cuckoo Round	15	Victorian Medley
7	The Skye Boat Song	16	La Bruja
8	Ua Like No a Like	17	Sentimental Medley
9	Scarborough Fair	18	Gymnopedie #1

Visit us on the Web at www.melbay.com — E-mail us at email@melbay.com

Introduction

The book you are holding grew out of my experience teaching at camps, festivals and workshops over the past few years. I kept hearing the same request: you wanted music you could play with a friend.

There is nothing quite like the wordless communication of playing music together. We musicians learn to listen for the subtle cues given by our fellow players, to synchronize our heart's rhythms to the beat, to breathe with the ebb and flow of the music.

As I was writing this book, I asked my students, friends and social media pals just what shape it should take. Most wanted arrangements for advancing beginners and intermediate players. Some asked for basic instruction on the ins and outs of using your fingers to play the uke; some wanted a challenge. Everyone wanted lyrics where appropriate. And all wanted a variety of material to stimulate that most intimate of relationships, the musical partnership.

I've done my best to fulfill all of these requirements with "Fingerstyle Duets for Ukulele." This book offers 21 songs arranged in 18 duets. The songs come from around the world: European waltzes, classical Hawaiian songs, folksongs, Victorian parlor pieces and classical guitar transcriptions.

Nothing in this book will be out of reach of the intermediate player. Advancing beginners will certainly find much here to help them achieve their musical goals. Even advanced players will find something to tickle their fancy.

As with my previous fingerstyle ukulele books, the arrangements get progressively more difficult as you move from the front to the back.

To help you get up to speed I've created eight basic fingerpicking exercises. If you have any questions about your ability to play fingerstyle ukulele, a little time spent here will pay off enormous dividends later on.

Including lyrics opens up many more possibilities: You could sing the melody while playing the accompaniment part. Add a vocal section to expand the duet arrangement. Or let the lyrics inform how you interpret the music as you play the arrangements as written.

The first four duets are designed as *etudes*, study pieces to help you build your skills. In each, the melody parts played by Ukulele 1 are quite simple and direct. Likewise, Ukulele 2 might play a single fingerpicking pattern for the first half of the song, switching to another pattern to finish.

You might notice that I've included extended arrangements of two of the songs from my Mel Bay book "Favorite Old Time American Songs for Ukulele." If you have that book – or view the short video lessons on my website – you will see how I transform a simple melody line into a full-fledged fingerstyle arrangement. Consider it a bonus lesson, or just enjoy playing a pair of time-honored American folk songs with a friend.

Later arrangements add more complexity: modulations, tricky harmonies, melodic variations, and twisty picking. Among these are two medleys right out of the Victorian parlor. Naturally, I've included a number of classic Hawaiian songs – nothing sounds better on this most Hawaiian musical instrument. The book concludes with my arrangement of Eric Satie's haunting solo piano piece "Gymnopedie #1," a fitting reward for all of your practice.

I hope you get as much enjoyment out of this book as I did in writing it.

Mark Kailana Nelson
Applegate Valley, Oregon
Spring, 2014
WWW.MARK-O.COM

Table of Contents

About the Tablature

All of the music is written in standard notation and tablature for ukulele.

Tablature, or TAB, is an ancient system of musical notation in which lines represent the instrument's strings. Fingering positions are indicated by numbers.

TAB doesn't give any indication of how long to hold each note; for that refer to the staff above the TAB. If you are unfamiliar with standard musical notation, see page 6.

Note that ukulele strings are numbered starting with the string closest to the floor, so A is the first string, E the second, C the third and G the fourth.

For reasons that are too complicated to go into here, TAB reverses the apparent order of the strings; A, the first string, appears as the top line of the TAB while the G string is on the bottom.

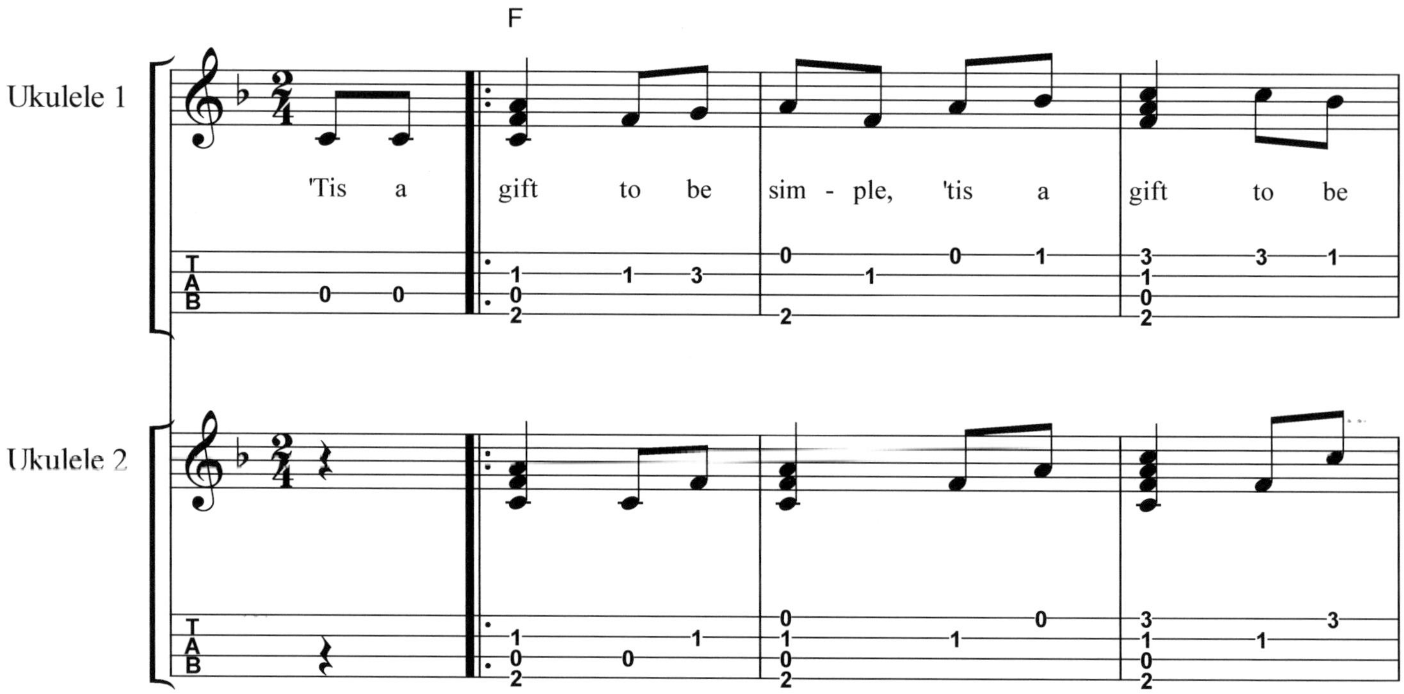

In general, Ukulele 1 plays the melody while Ukulele 2 handles the accompaniment and harmony, though in a few arrangements they swap roles over the course of the song.

Wherever practical, use the chord symbols to pre-set your fingers; most of the melody and accompaniment falls directly out of the common chord shapes.

In the example above, for the pickup measure, Ukulele 1 plays two eighth notes on the open C string. In Measure 2, play the F chord by pinching the 2nd, 3rd and 4th strings with your thumb and two fingers. Then play single notes as indicated.

Ukulele 2 rests for the pickup measure. Notice that the downbeat of the first measure is played the same way as Ukulele 1; as a pinch on strings 2, 3 and 4. The two single notes are played while holding down the F chord.

If you need a refresher on how to play with your fingers, see page 8.

Here are some more TAB symbols and playing techniques you will encounter.

Slide: Pick the first note – or notes – and then slide up or down to the second. Be sure to give each note its full time value!

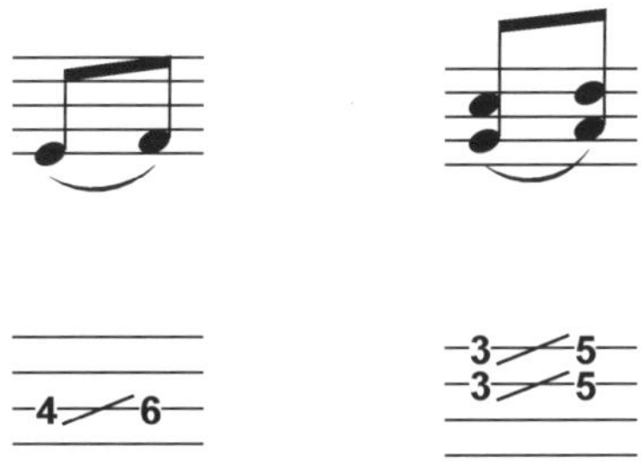

Hammer-on: Play the first note, then rapidly press your finger down to the fretboard to sound the second note.

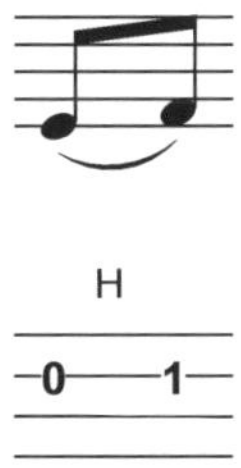

Pull-off: Play the first note, then quickly pull off your finger to sound the lower note.

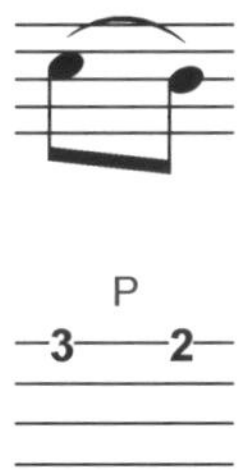

Hammer/pull combination: A rapid combination of a hammer-on and pull-off executed as a quick flick of the finger.

A Very Brief Word About Musical Notation

Since the TAB will give you the correct pitches on a properly tuned instrument, it is not necessary to know how to read music to play through this book.

However, knowledge of a few musical symbols will help find your way around the arrangements. This brief introduction is no substitute for serious study – as with any other language skill, reading music requires much practice and patience. Fortunately, there is no shortage of resources waiting your discovery.

Here are a few common musical symbols defined.

Music is divided into **measures**, each of which contains the number of beats delineated by the **time signature**:

4/4 means four beats per measure, each quarter note counts as one beat.

3/4 is three beats per measure, each quarter note counts as one beat.

Occasionally alternate symbols are used for the time signature. **Common Time**  is the same as 4/4.

Each beat can be further divided into smaller and smaller units:

The longest note is the whole note; it is the equivalent of four quarter notes.

The half note is equal to two quarter notes.

The quarter note gets one count in 4/4 time.

Two eighth notes equal a quarter note.

The sixteenth note is half as long as the eighth note; so two sixteenths equal one eighth, four sixteenths equal a quarter, and sixteen equal a whole note.

Rests correspond to each of the different note values.

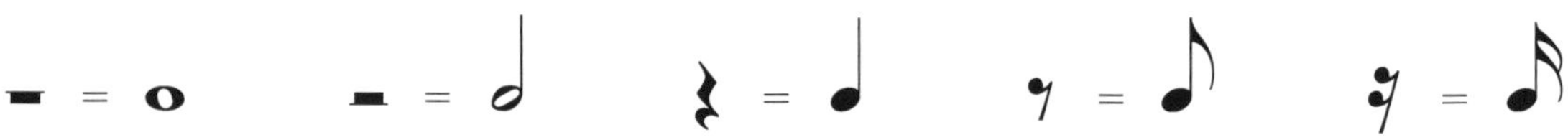

A dot placed next to a note (or rest) lengthens it by one half of its value. 

Ties are used for notes that are held for their combined values. 

Triplets are groups of three notes that are played in the space of two. These eighth note triplets would be played in the same amount of time as two eighth notes.

Music tends to repeat itself. Rather than copying and pasting large numbers of identical measures, arrangers use the following signs and symbols as shortcuts for navigation.

Repeat signs: Repeat the enclosed phrase one time before going on to the next one.

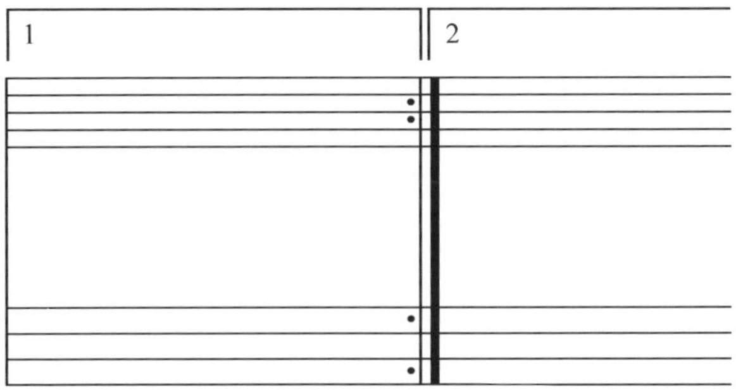

First/Second Endings: Play the measures up to the repeat on the first time through and then go back to the beginning of the section. On the repeat you skip over the first ending and play the second ending.

D.C. From the Italian, **Da Capo**, meaning "Head." This sign directs you to go back to the beginning of the music. **D.C. al Fine** directs you to play from the beginning to the end of the song. **D.C. al Coda** means play from the beginning to the coda sign, then jump to the coda.

D.S. **Dal Segno**, or "to the sign," tells you to look for the symbol (𝄋) and play that section next rather than returning to the beginning. D.S. al Coda means play from the sign to the coda sign, then jump to the coda.

𝄌 A **Coda** sign marks the ending of the piece. When you see **To Coda**, skip down to the section with the coda sign to finish the song. *Coda* is Italian for "Tail," by the way.

Basic Fingerpicking Exercises

Fingerpicking comes in many forms and flavors. At the most basic, the term refers to playing individual strings with the fingers of your right hand – or left, for lefties. Thus it differs from strumming or the more basic single note plucking using the thumb or forefinger practiced by many ukulele players.

If you are new to the whole concept, here are some simple exercises to get you going. Master these, and the rest of the book will be a snap.

To begin, hold your picking hand in front of you and relax your wrist. Notice how your fingers naturally curl slightly as they point towards the floor? Wiggle your thumb and fingers a bit, bringing them in towards your palm. Congratulations, you have just discovered the optimal hand position for fingerpicking.

Example 1:

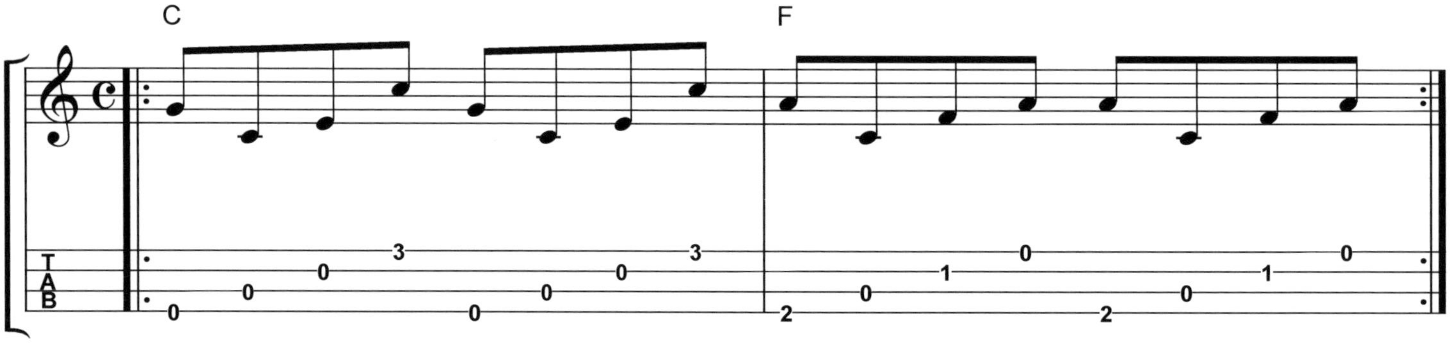

Starting with your thumb on the G string, place one finger on each string. Remember to relax, and keep your fingers slightly bowed. If you need to, rest your pinky on the face of the uke to steady your hand.

Hold a simple C chord, and pick the strings in this order: thumb, index, middle, ring. Try to keep a steady rhythm. After four beats, change to an F chord and repeat the same motion. Continue until the motions feel natural.

In classical guitar, your fingers are given abbreviations *p-i-m-a* based on their Spanish names: *pulgar* (thumb), *índice* (index finger), *medio* (middle finger), *anular* (ring finger).

Example 2:

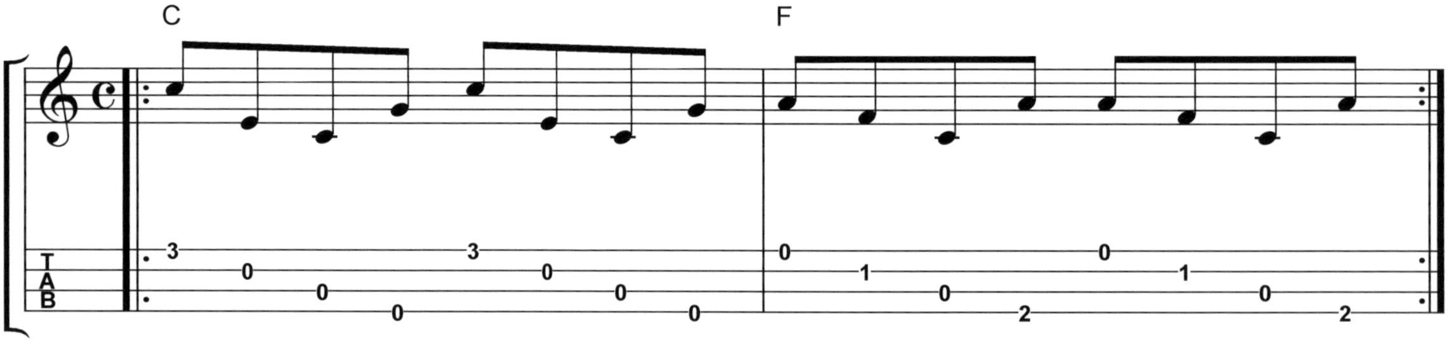

As you can see, this is the opposite motion from the previous exercise. Set your fingers as before: thumb on the G string and one finger per string. While holding the C and F chords, pick each string in succession beginning with your ring finger: ring, middle, index, thumb. (Or *a - m - i - p*)

As with any exercise, the key is to take your time. Play as slowly as you need in order not to make a mistake. Over time, gradually pick up speed, above all keeping the rhythm steady. When you feel confident, try using these patterns over different chords.

Example 3:

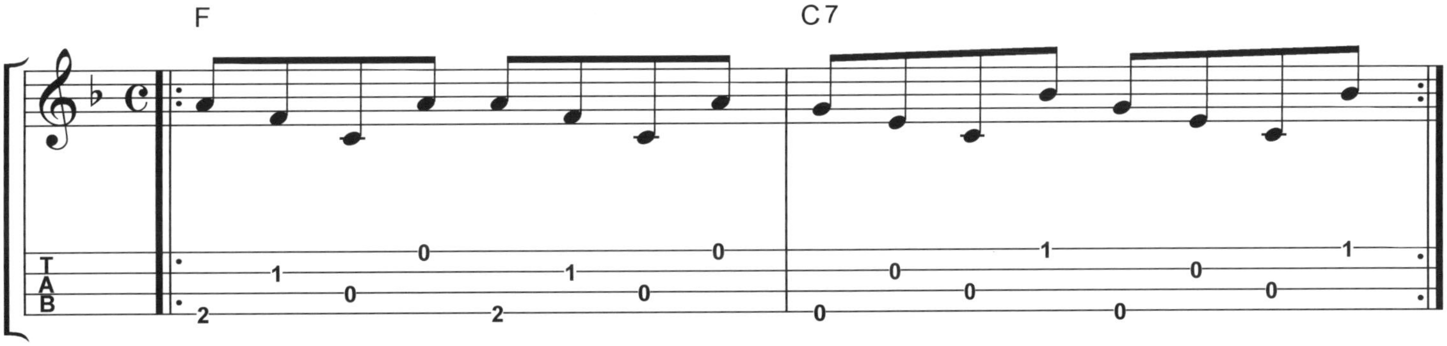

Set up your fingers as before. While holding down an F chord, pluck the strings in this order: Thumb, middle, index, ring (or *p-m-i-a*). Play the pattern twice, then switch to a C7 chord and repeat. For this and the next few exercises, it may be useful to say the names of the fingers out loud as you practice. Repeat both measures until it feels easy.

Example 4:

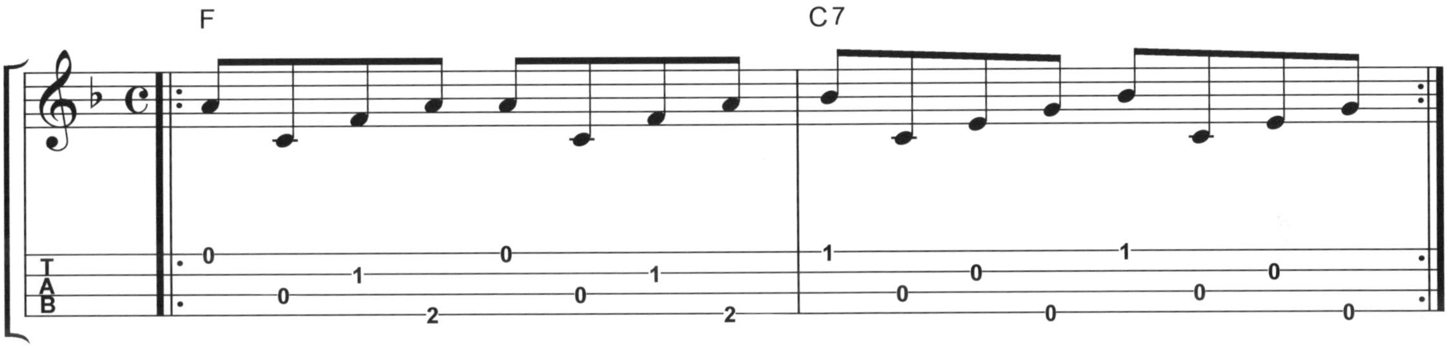

This pattern also uses alternate fingers to pick the strings. While holding down F and C7 chords, pick with your ring finger, index, middle and thumb (*a - i - m - p*). Again, saying the names of your fingers out loud may help sort through any confusion.

Example 5:

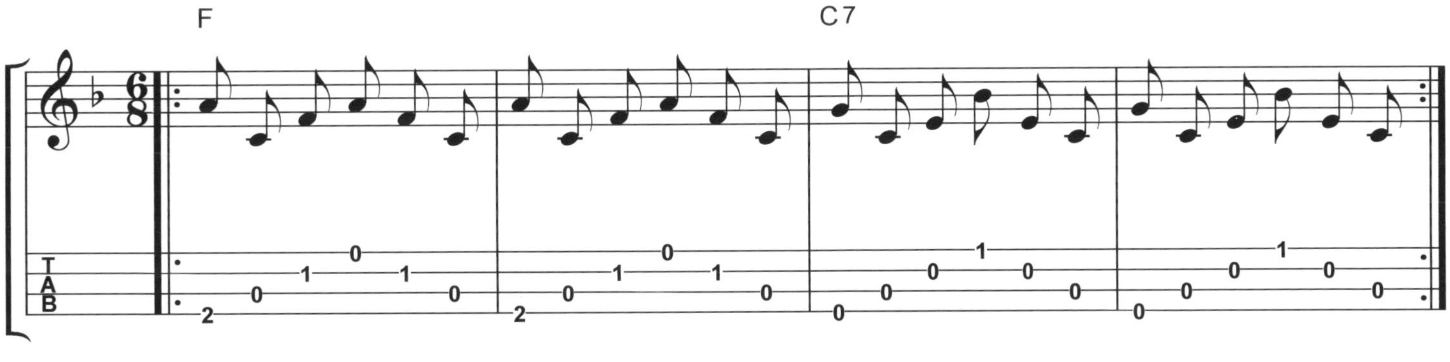

Note the change to 6/8 time. This is essentially the first two patterns combined: *p- i- m - a - m - i* (or thumb-index-middle-ring-middle-index) against F and C7 chords. The effect is quite lovely and fits well with many kinds of music in triple meter.

"Pattern Picking," as this style is called, is a powerful tool to have at your command. Once you feel you have mastered these examples, try applying them to songs that you already have in your repertoire.

As you begin working through the arrangements, you will find numerous examples where one or the other ukulele uses repeated patterns.

Next we'll take a look at some other fingerpicking techniques that lend themselves to both accompaniment and melodic playing.

Example 6:

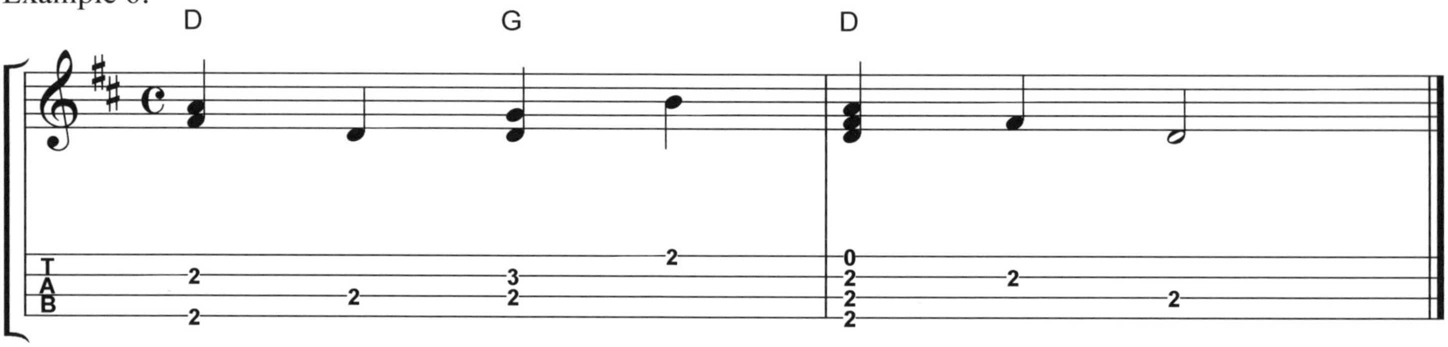

When you pick two or more strings together using your thumb and fingers, it's a called a pinch. Play the first pinch with your thumb and middle finger; use your index for the next note. The second double-stop (another name for playing two notes at once) is index and middle, followed by the ring finger. Pinch all four strings for the full chord and round out the measure with the ring and index fingers.

Example 7:

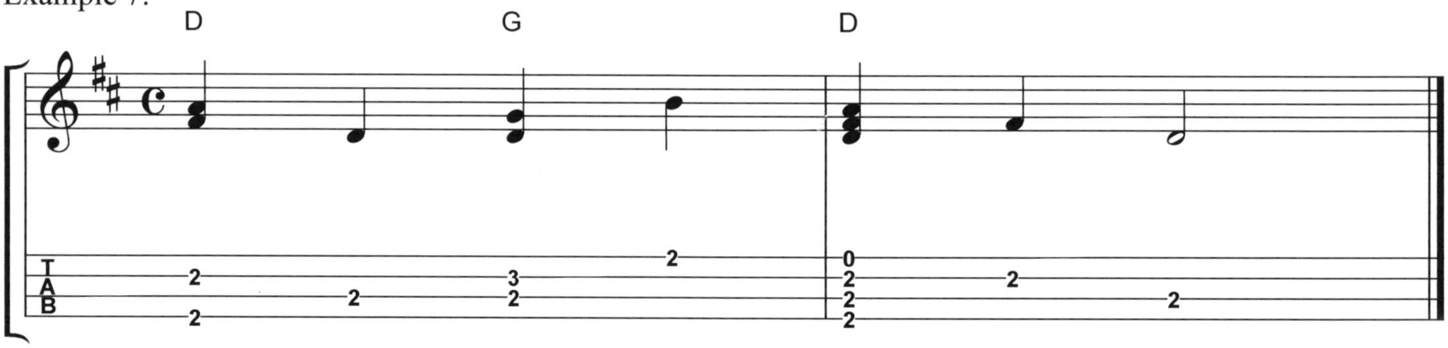

Yep, it looks exactly the same as the previous one. But instead of setting up with one-finger-per-string as you've done previously, your thumb takes a more active role. Play the first pinch using your thumb and index finger. Move your thumb down to the third string for the next note.

Play the second pinch with your thumb and index finger, followed by the note on the first string with your middle finger.

Play the chord, then add the next two notes with your index finger and thumb. The chord may be played either as a four note pinch, a downward strum, or even an upward strum!

Example 8:

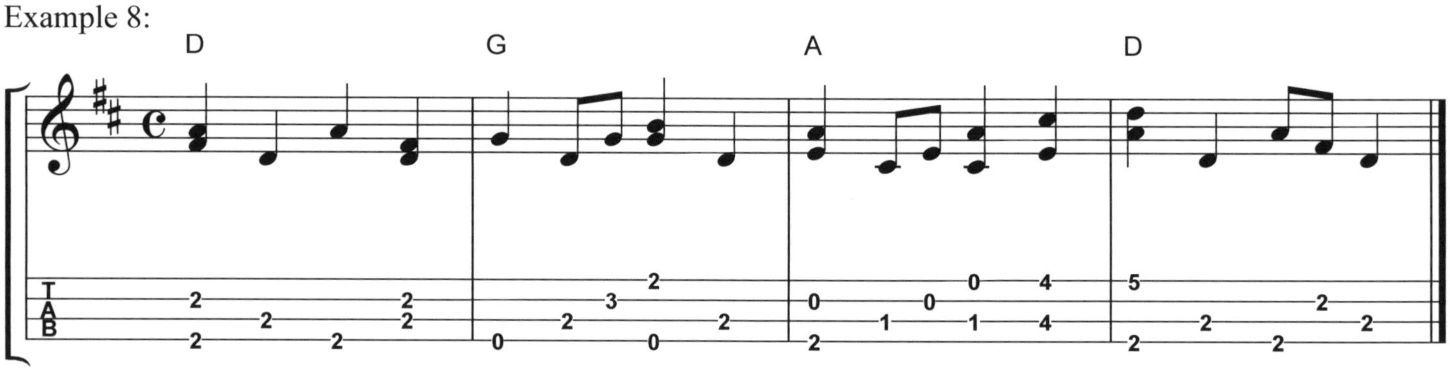

This last exercise introduces alternating-thumb picking. Also called "Travis Picking," after the great guitarist Merle Travis, this style lends itself well to playing melody while keeping a steady beat. It is not easy to learn, but well worth it.

Play all of the notes on strings three and four with your thumb and use your index and ring fingers for any notes on the first and second strings. Note that notes that fall on the beat are played with the thumb, either alone or as pinches with one or more fingers. Notes on the off beats are always played with fingers alone.

In Measure 3, your thumb slips out of the steady alternating pattern.

The previous exercises are just some of the ways to play ukulele using your fingers. As you progress through the arrangements, feel free to experiment and make up your own approach.

Fingerstyle Duets for Ukulele

The first few arrangements are *etudes*, studies designed to get you comfortable playing ukulele duets. They offer a taste of many of the techniques and styles that follow. If you have never played fingerstyle before, I'd suggest learning the four *etudes* in the order given. For these first arrangements, neither part should offer too much of a challenge to advancing beginners and intermediate players.

The accompaniment in the first four songs most often follows a basic pattern picking style for a number of measures, sometimes with subtle variations thrown in for effect. Similarly, the melodic parts tend to start out simple and get only slightly more complex as the arrangement progresses. Within a short time you will encounter all of the techniques you'll find later on.

In the latter arrangements, I have kept to the general pattern where Ukulele 1 carries the melody while Ukulele 2 handles accompaniment chores. Though, to be sure, I did change things up a bit every now and then.

The arrangements become more difficult as you move from front to back. As you progress, you and your musical partner might want to swap parts from time to time. Nothing like a little variety to keep things interesting.

I purposely did not indicate tempo; rather let your sense of how the song should sound best be your guide. Some pieces – such as Gymnopedie #1 – sound best at a languid tempo; others can stand a more sprightly approach.

So find a partner, tune up and get ready to play some great ukulele duets.

Sicilian Waltz

Track 1

Traditional Italian

C
G7
1.
Uke 1
Uke 2
C
2.
C7
F
Uke 1
Uke 2

C
G7
17
Uke 1
Uke 2

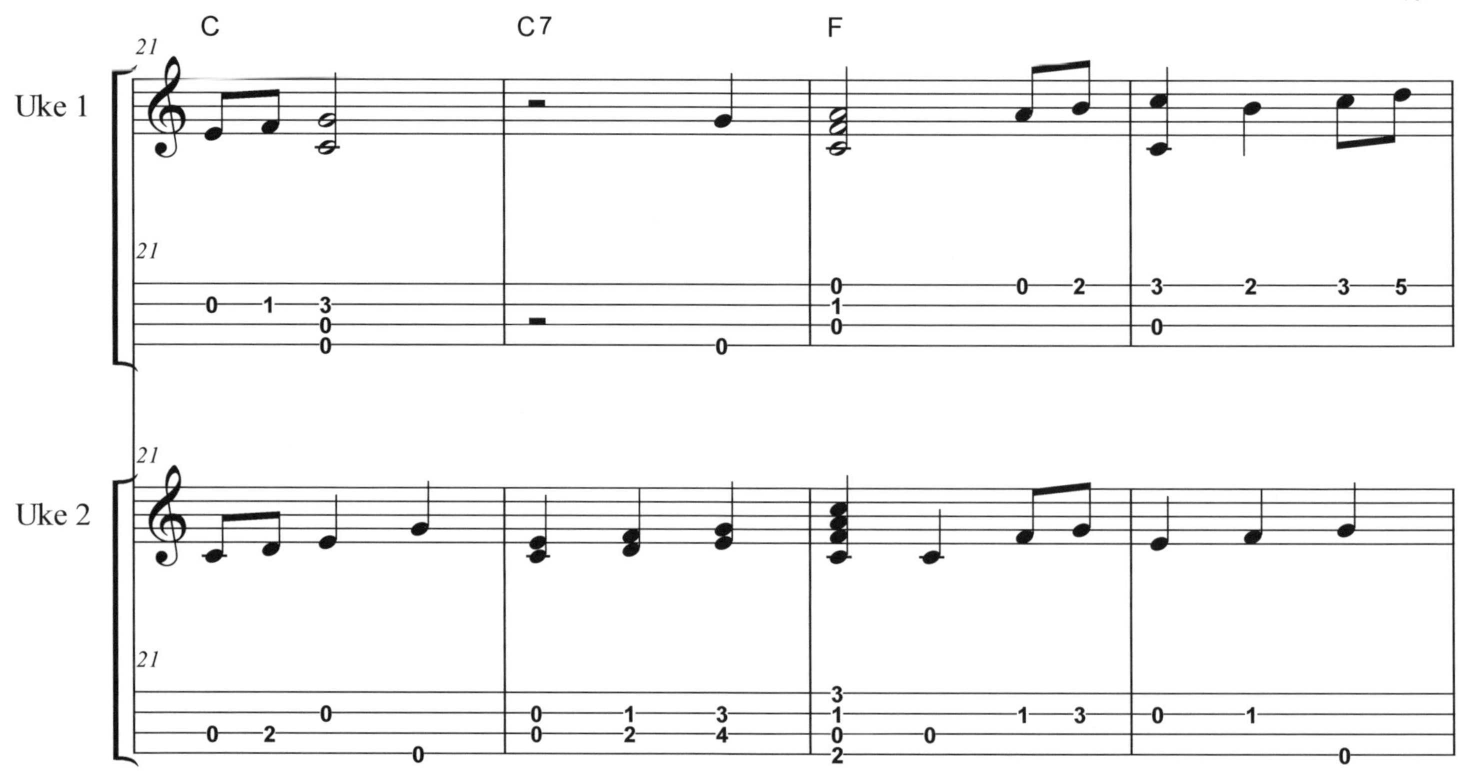
C
C7
F
21
Uke 1
Uke 2

C
G7
Uke 1
Uke 2
C
G7
D.S. al Fine
C
rit.
G7
C
Uke 1
Uke 2

Simple Gifts

Track 2

Joseph Brackett

F
Uke 1
be, And when we find our - selves in the place just
Uke 2
C7 F B♭
Uke 1
right, We will be in the val - ley of love and de -
Uke 2

F
Uke 1
light. When true sim - pli - ci - ty is
Uke 2
C7
Uke 1
gained, To bow and to bend we will not be a -
Uke 2

Uke 1
Uke 2
F
shamed. To turn, turn, will be our de - light, Till by
C F B♭ F F
1. 2.
turn - ing, turn - ing we come round right.

The Banks of the Ohio

Track 3

Traditional American

Uke 1
Uke 2
D D A7
day. On-ly say that you'll be mine And in my home, we'll hap-py
D G D A7
be Down be - side, where the wa-ters flow, Down by the banks of the O-hi-

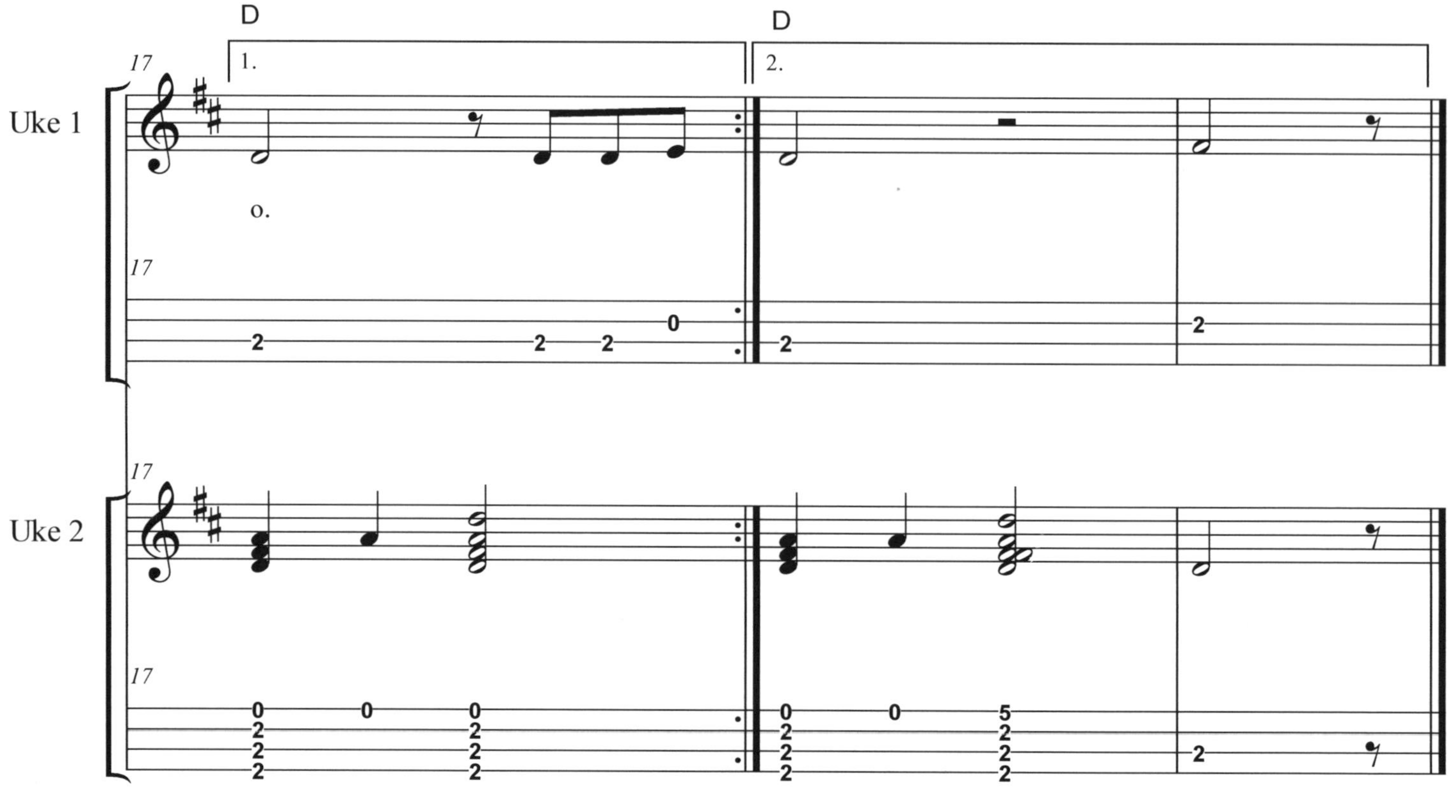
D
D
1.
2.
17
Uke 1
Uke 2

The Banks of the Ohio

I asked my love to take a walk,
Just to walk a little way,
As we walk, oh may we talk
All about our wedding day.

Chorus
Only say that you'll be mine,
And in my home we'll happy be,
Down beside, where the waters flow,
Down by the banks of the Ohio.

I held my knife against her breast,
As into my arms she pressed.
She said, "Willie, don't you murder me
I'm unprepared for eternity."

I took her by her lily-white hand,
And dragged her down that bank of sand,
And there I pushed her in to drown,
And I watched her as she floated down.

I came home at half past one,
I cried, "My God, what have I done?"
I killed the only girl I love
Because she would not marry me.

The very next day, at half past four,
The sheriff knocked upon my door,
Sayin', "Young man, it's time to go,
Down to the banks of the Ohio."

Margaret's Waltz

Track 4

Traditional English

A
1.
A
2.
C♯m
F♯m
Uke 1
Uke 2
D
E7
F♯m
C♯m
Uke 1
Uke 2

D
E7
A
F♯m
Uke 1
Uke 2
Bm
E7
A
To Coda 27
F♯m
Uke 1
Uke 2

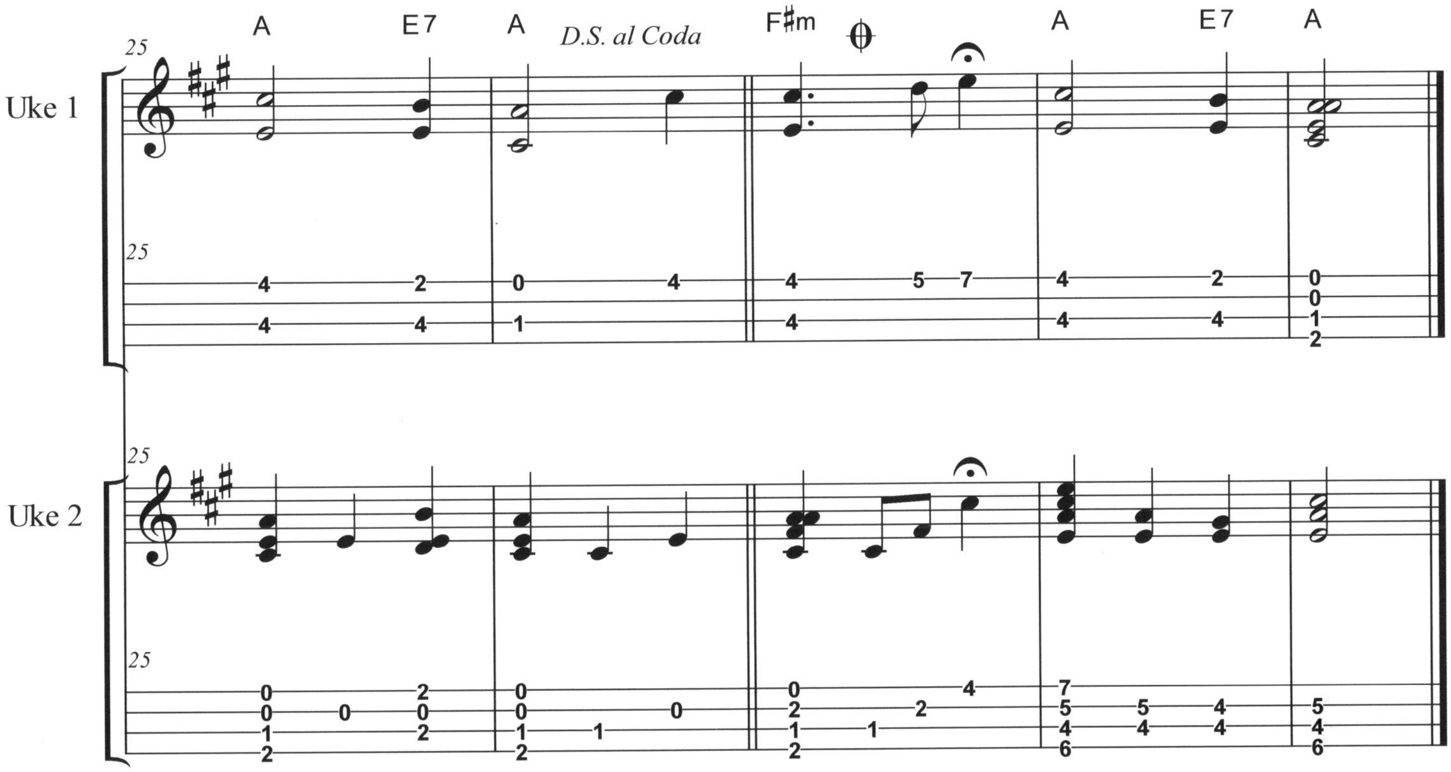
A E7 A D.S. al Coda F♯m A E7 A
Uke 1
Uke 2

Ahi Wela

Track 5

Lizzie Doirin & Mary Beckley

C F C G7
Uke 1
poli A - hi wela mai ne - i lo - ko I ka han - a ke a -
Uke 2

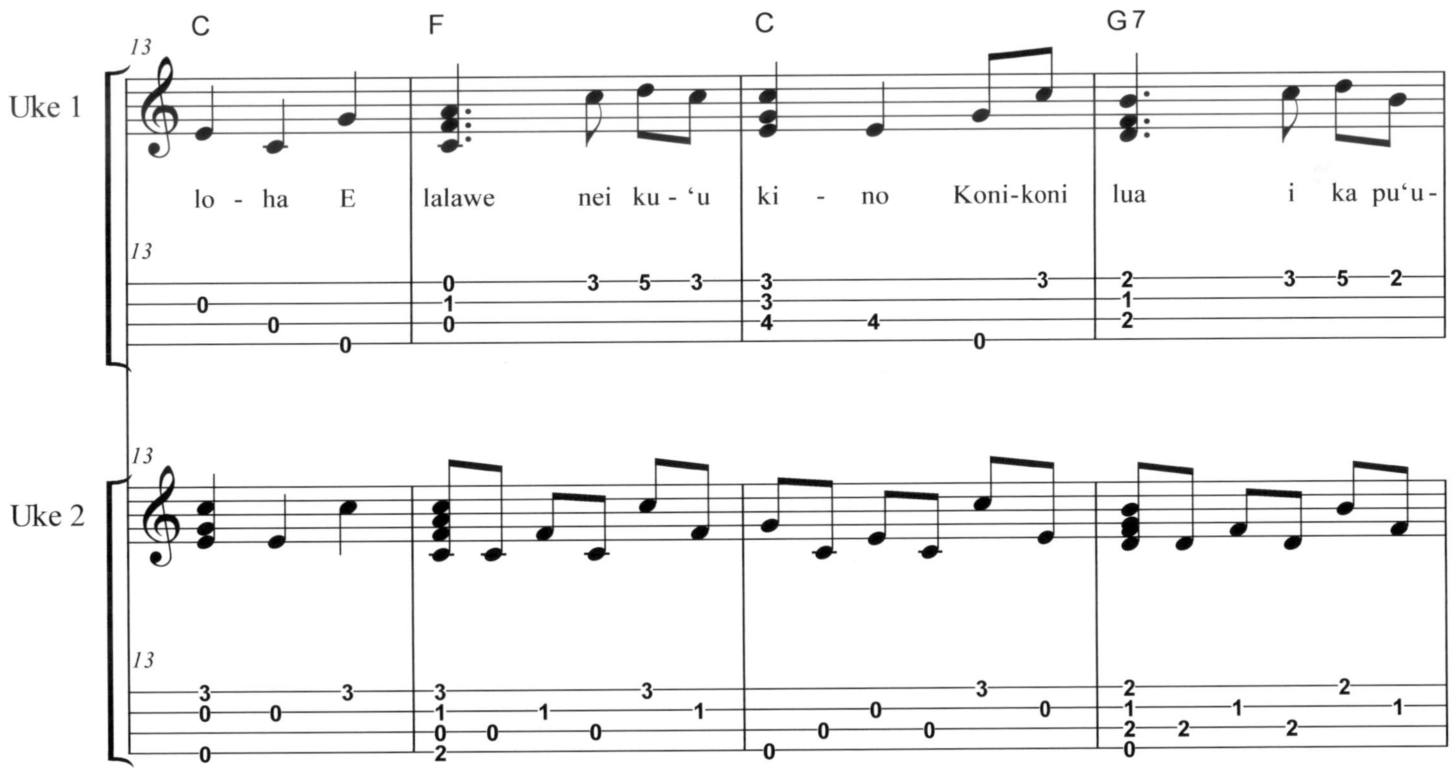
C F C G7
Uke 1
lo - ha E lalawe nei ku - ‘u ki - no Koni-koni lua i ka pu‘u -
Uke 2

A ʻelua nō māua
I ʻike ia hana
Laʻi wale ke kāunu
Hoʻonipo i ka poli

Hui
Ahi wela mai nei loko
I ka hana a ke aloha
E lalawe nei kuʻu kino
Konikoni lua i ka puʻuwai

ʻAuhea wale ana ʻoe
Kuʻu pua i kui a lei
I lei hoʻohiehie
Nō ke anu ahiahi

Kuʻu pua i liʻa ai
Aʻu i kui ai a lawa
I lei hoʻohiehie
Nō ke ano ahiahi

Elua nō māua
A i ʻike ia hana
Laʻi ai ka nanea ʻana
Hoʻonipo i kuʻu kino

There were two of us
Who knew about it.
The acts of love
There within the heart

Chorus
Like a hot fire inside,
The act of love
Is going through my body
And throbbing in my heart.

Where are you,
My flower that I strung into a lei?
A lei to adorn me
In the cool evening.

My flower, for which I yearn
I have strung and made
An elegant lei
In the coolness of the evening.

There were two of us
Who knew about it.
Peacefully relaxing;
Making love.

The Cuckoo Round

Track 6

Traditional French

C C C
Uke 1
Uke 2
G7 C C C
Uke 1
Uke 2

G7
C
C
1.
2.
D.S. al Fine
Uke 1
Uke 2
18

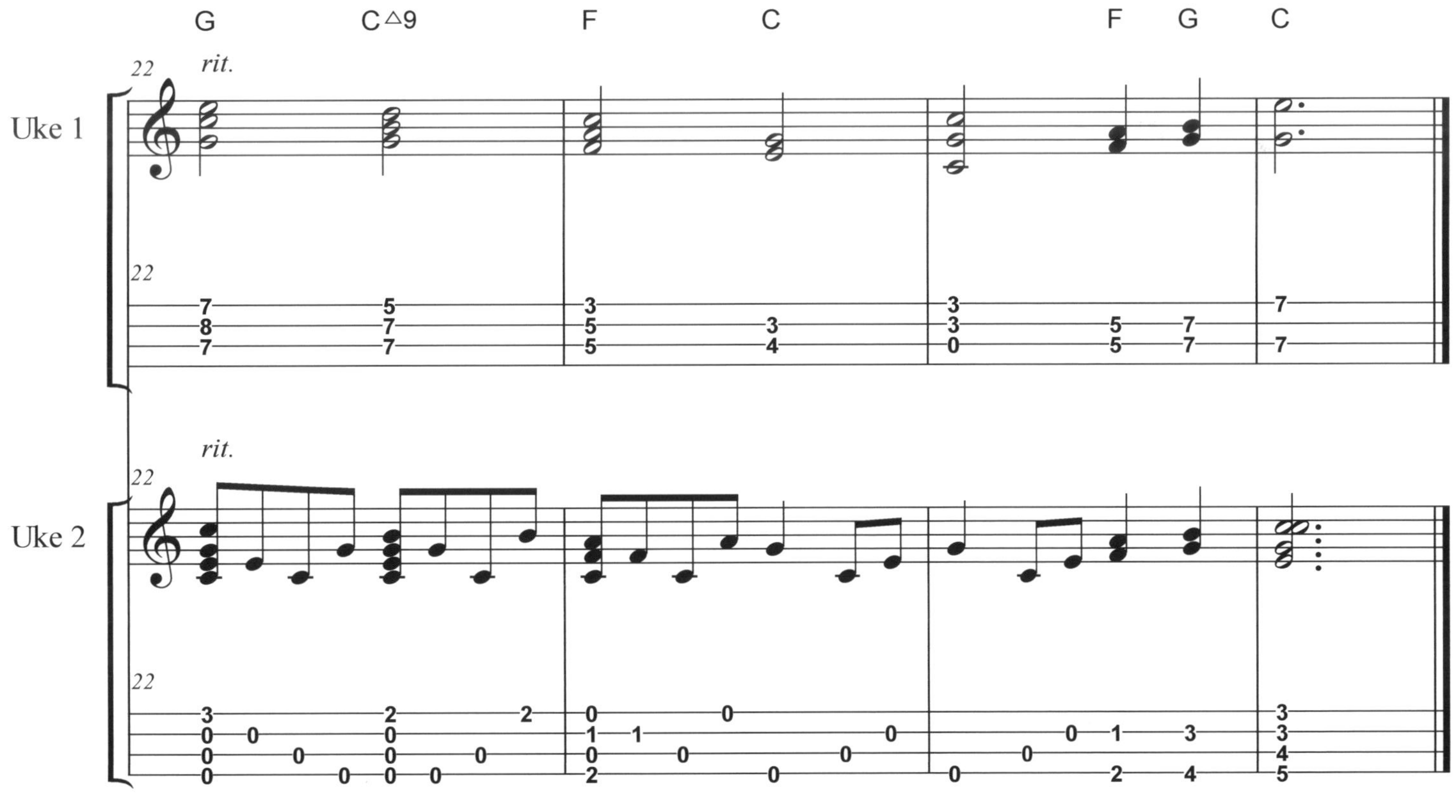
G
C△9
F
C
F
G
C
rit.
Uke 1
Uke 2
22

The Skye Boat Song

Track 7

Traditional Scottish

D Em Am Em
Uke 1
Skye.
Loud the winds howl, loud the waves roar, Thun - der clouds rent the
Uke 2
C D Em7 Am Em
Uke 1
air;
Baf - fled our foes stand by the shore, Fol - low they will not
Uke 2

16
Uke 1
Uke 2
C
C G
C Am Dm Em7
1.
2.
dare.
20
Am F C G C Am Dm G

Am
F
C
G
Am
Dm
24
Uke 1
Uke 2

Am
F
Am
Dm
28
Uke 1
Uke 2

The Skye Boat Song

Speed bonny boat, like a bird on the wing,
Onward, the sailors cry;
Carry the lad that's born to be king
Over the sea to Skye.

Loud the winds howl, loud the waves roar,
Thunder clouds rent the air;
Baffled our foes, stand by the shore,
Follow they will not dare.

Though the waves leap, soft shall ye sleep,
The ocean's a royal bed.
Rock in the deep, Flora will keep
Watch on your weary head.

Many's the lad fought on that day,
Well the claymore could wield,
When the night came, silently lay,
Dead on Culloden's Field.

Burned are our homes, exile and death
Scatter the loyal men;
Yet ere that sword cool in the sheath
Charlie will come again.

Ua Like No a Like

Track 8

Alice Everett

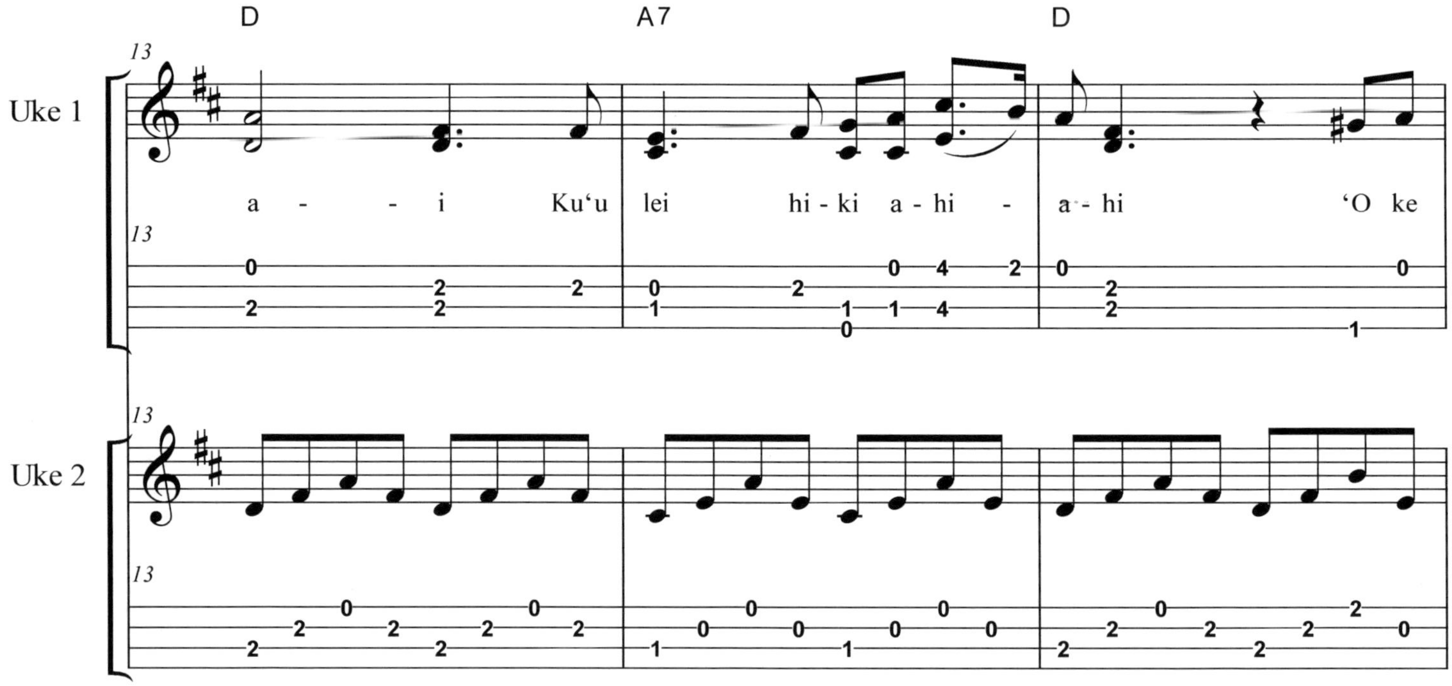

Ua like nō a like
Me ka ua kani lehua
Me he ala e ‘i mai ana
Aia i laila ke aloha

Hui
‘O ‘oe nō ka‘u i ‘upu ai
Ku‘u lei hiki ahiahi
‘O ke kani a nā manu
I nā hola o ke aumoe

Ma ‘anei mai kāua
He welina pa‘a i ka poli
A nāu nō au e ‘imi a‘e
A loa`a i ke aheahe a ka makani

He moani ka‘u i honi
‘Oiai eia i ka midnight
Me na kipona waianuhea
Ka ma‘alo a‘e i kuu maka

It is like the rain
That falls on the lehua blossom.
It seems to be saying
"Love is there."

We are here together
With a love that binds us both.
So let me seek you
Where the gentle breezes blow.

Chorus
You are the one I'm thinking of;
My beloved who comes in the evening,
When you hear the birdsong
And the night has fallen.

I smell a wind-borne perfume
Here at midnight,
Amid subtle fragrances
Wafting around me.

Scarborough Fair

Track 9

Traditional English

Uke 1
Uke 2
B♭ F C Dm G
Re-mem - ber me to one who lives there, For she once was a
C Dm C C B♭ A Dm
1. 2.
true love of mine.

18
C
Dm
G
Dm
B♭
Uke 1
Uke 2
22
F
C
Dm
G
C
Dm
Uke 1
Uke 2

Scarborough Fair

Are you going to Scarborough Fair?
Parsley, sage, rosemary and thyme
Remember me to one who lives there,
For she once was a true love of mine.

Tell her to make me a cambric shirt
Parsley, sage, rosemary and thyme
Without a seam nor needlework,
And then she'll be a true love of mine.

Tell her to wash it in yonder dry well.
Where never spring water or rain ever fell,
And she shall be a true love of mine.

Tell her to find me an acre of land
Between the salt water and the sea strands
Then she'll be a true love of mine

Tell her to reap it with a sickle of leather
Parsley sage rosemary and thyme
And gather it all in a bunch of heather
Then she'll be a true love of mine

‘Akaka Falls

Track 10

Helen Parker

C9
F
F7
Uke 1
Uke 2
B♭6
Dm7
Uke 1
Uke 2

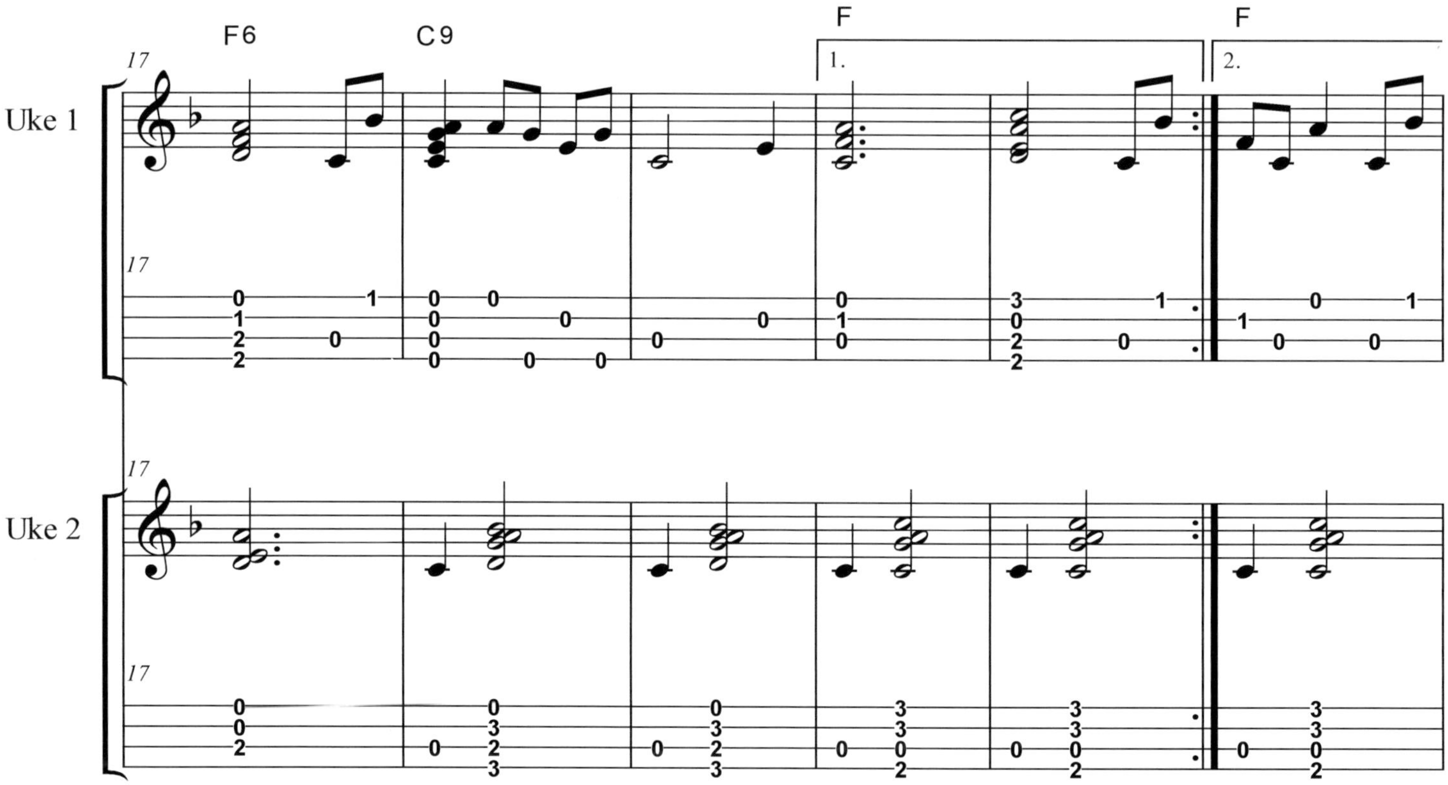
F6
C9
F
F
1.
2.
Uke 1
Uke 2

C9
F
D♭
Uke 1
Uke 2

E♭
F
D♭
Uke 1
Uke 2
E♭
F
F M9
Uke 1
Uke 2

Hard Times, Come Again No More

Track 11

Stephen Foster

D Bm A7 D G F♯m Bm A7 D
Uke 1
song that will lin-ger for - ev-er in our ears; Oh hard times come a-gain no more. Tis the
Uke 2

F♯m Bm G F♯m Bm G D F♯m A7
Uke 1
song, the sigh of the wear - y, Hard Times, hard times, come a-gain no more Man-y
Uke 2

D Bm Em D G D A7 D A7
1.
Uke 1
days you have ling-ered a - round my ca-bin door; Oh hard times come a-gain no more.
Uke 2
D Dsus D G D A7 D Dsus D
2.
Uke 1
Uke 2

Hard Times, Come Again No More

Let us pause in life's pleasures and count its many tears,
While we all sup sorrow with the poor;
There's a song that will linger forever in our ears;
Oh hard times come again no more.

Chorus
Tis the song, the sigh of the weary,
Hard Times, hard times, come again no more
Many days you have lingered around my cabin door;
Oh hard times come again no more.

While we seek mirth and beauty and music light and gay,
There are frail forms fainting at the door;
Though their voices are silent, their pleading looks will say
Oh hard times come again no more.

There's a pale drooping maiden who toils her life away,
With a worn heart whose better days are o'er:
Though her voice would be merry, 'tis sighing all the day,
Oh hard times come again no more.

Tis a sigh that is wafted across the troubled wave,
Tis a wail that is heard upon the shore
Tis a dirge that is murmured around the lowly grave
Oh hard times come again no more.

Fandanguillo

Track 12

Traditional Spanish

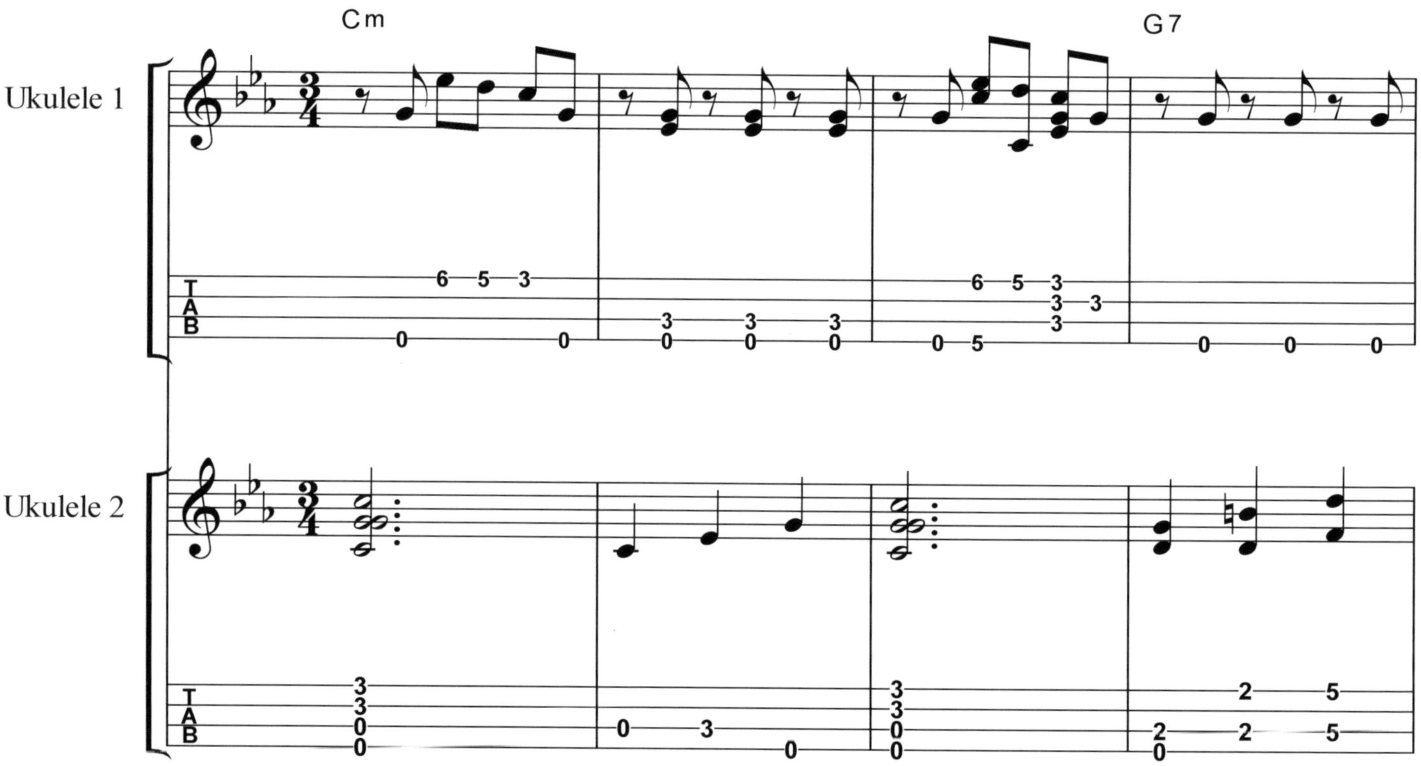

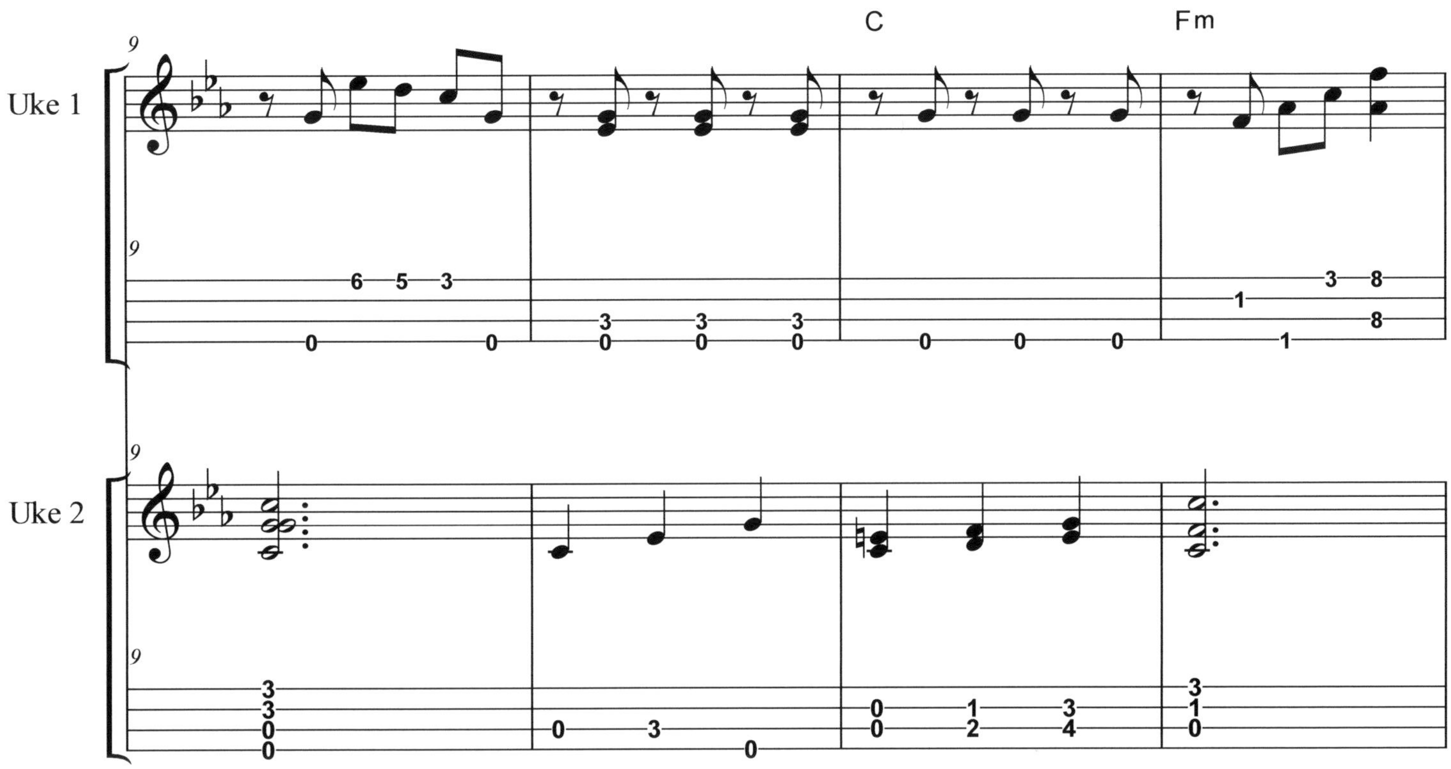
Uke 1
Uke 2
C
Fm

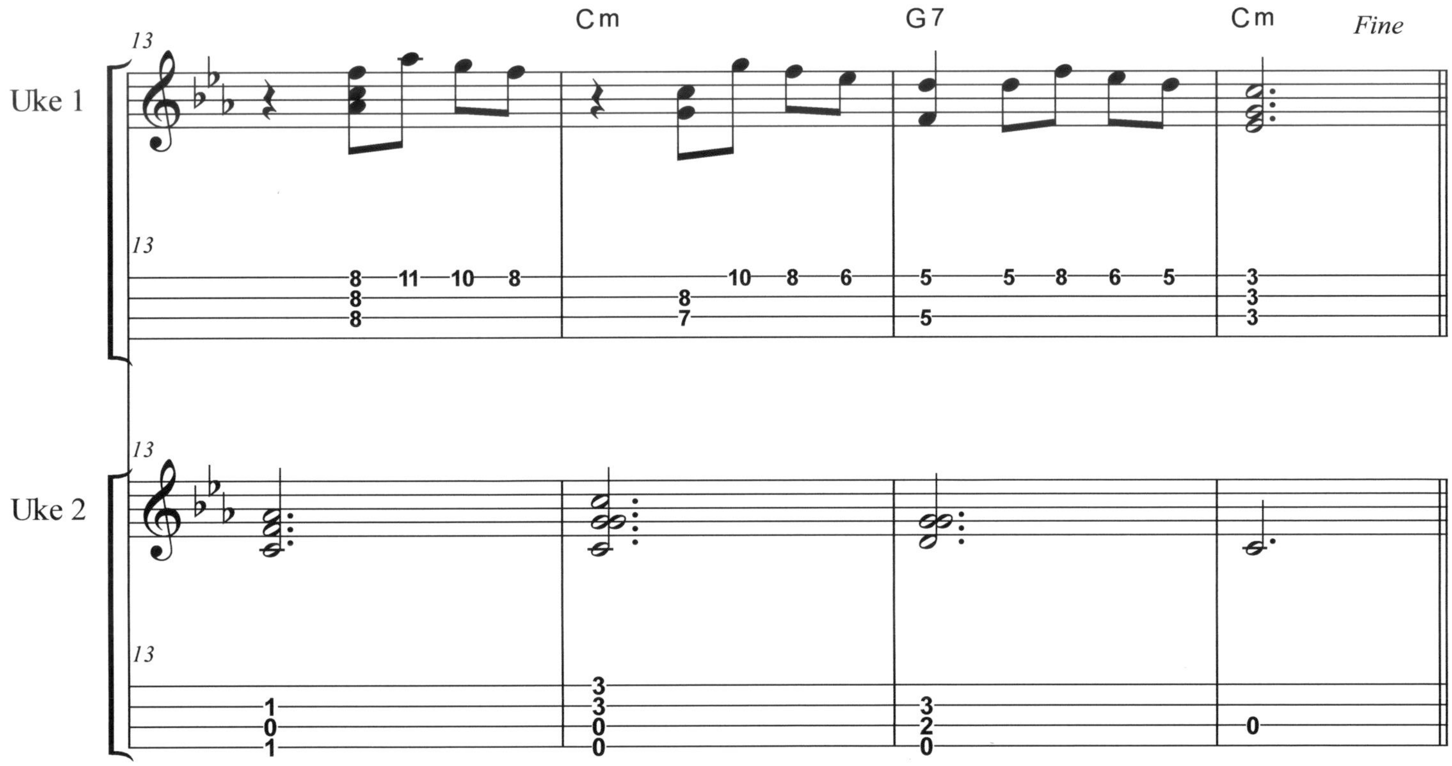
Uke 1
Uke 2
Cm
G7
Cm
Fine

G7
Cm
17
Uke 1
Uke 2

G7
Cm
21
Uke 1
Uke 2

Uke 1
Uke 2
G7
Cm
B♭
A♭
G7
A♭dim
D.C. al Fine

Home Sweet Home

Track 13

Henry Bishop & Howard Payne

F B♭ F B♭ C7 F F♯dim Gm C7
Uke 1
home; A charm from the skies seems to hal - low us
Uke 2
F B♭ C7 F F♯dim Gm C7
Uke 1
there, Which seek thro' the world, is ne'er met with else -
Uke 2

F F C7 Dm C7
Uke 1
where. Home! Home! Sweet, sweet
Uke 2

F B♭ C7 F6 F♯dim Gm6 C7
Uke 1
home! There's no place like home There's no place like
Uke 2

F C7 F F♯dim Gm C7
Uke 1
home!
Uke 2
F B♭6 F
Uke 1
Uke 2

Sweet Lei Lehua

Track 14

King David Kalākaua

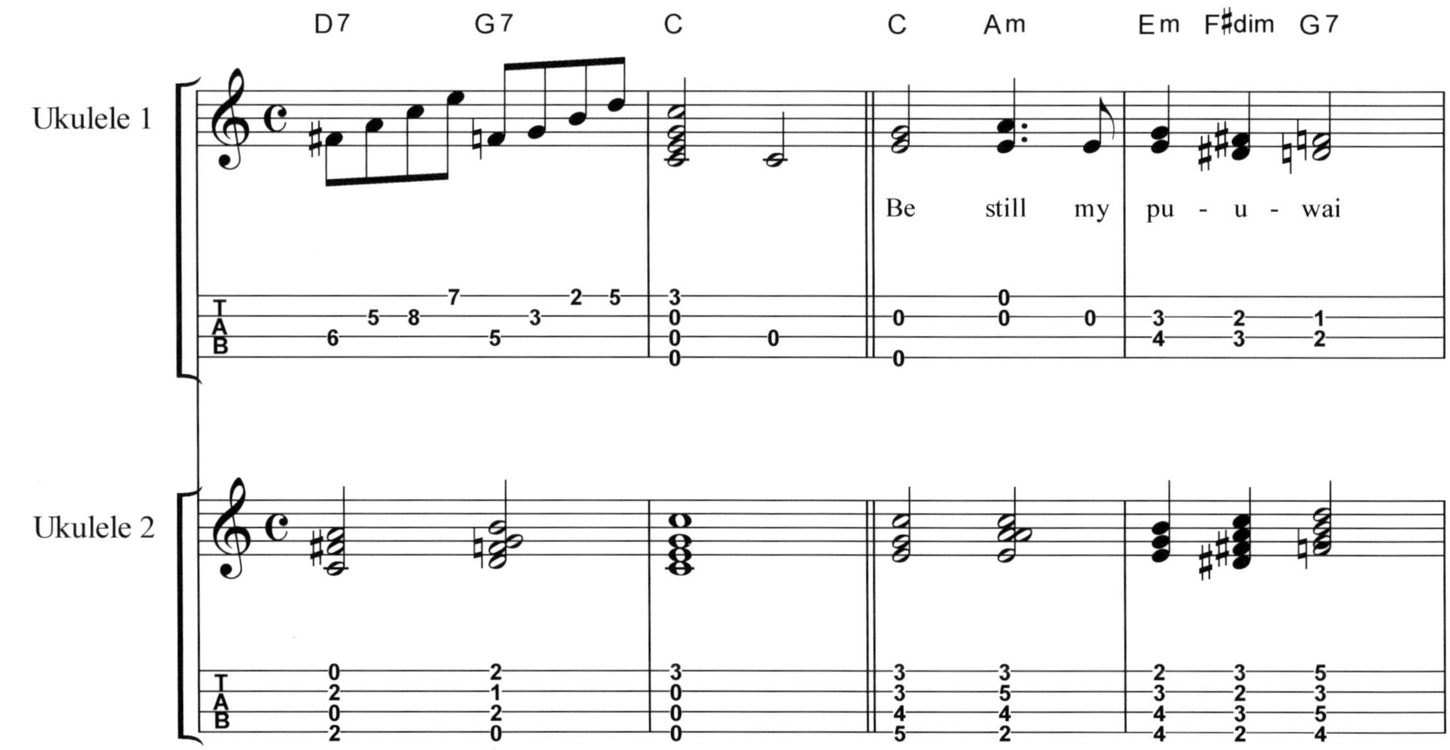

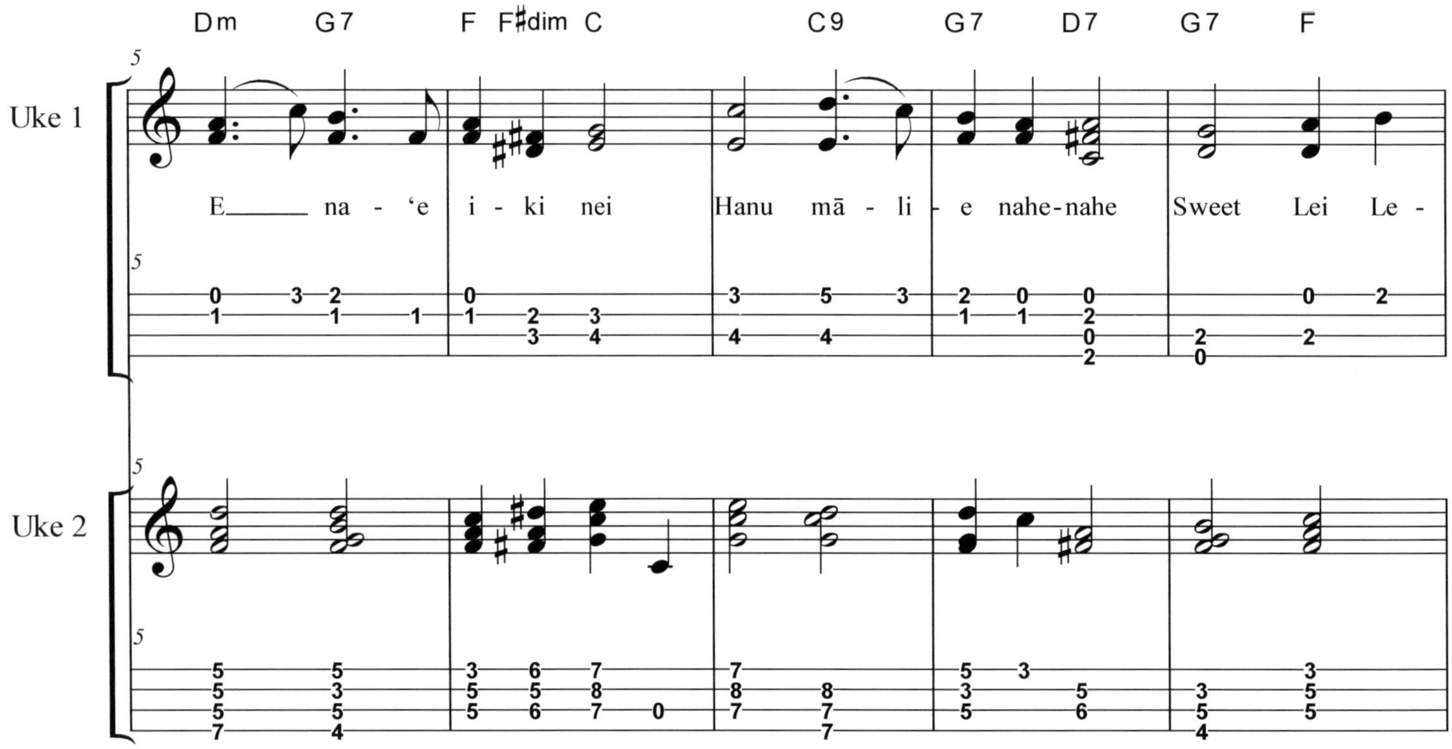

G7 C G7 C C Am Em F♯dim G7
Uke 1
hu - a
Uke 2
Dm G9 C6 C7 G7 D7 G7 F
Uke 1
Uke 2

Be still my pu‘uwai
E na‘e iki nei
Hanu mālie nahenahe
Sweet lei lehua

Ho’olale mai ‘oe ku‘u mana‘o
Moe uhane wau ia ‘oe a ku‘u aloha
I ke awakea me ke ahiahi
Ku‘u lei lehua a‘ala

Hui
Kāpa‘a ‘oe e ka‘u mea nani
Kūpa‘a me au kau pule ke ia
Ha‘awi mai ‘oe kou lima i‘au
Ku‘u lei lehua a‘ala

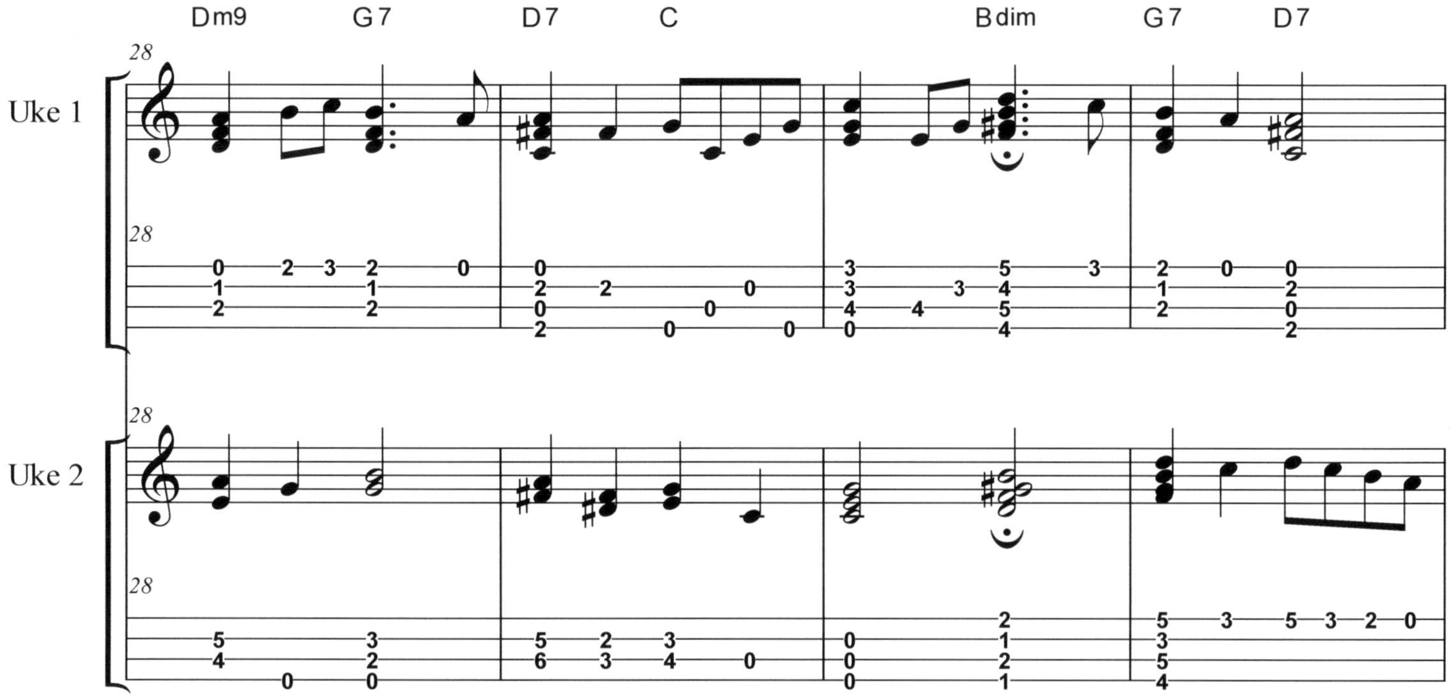

Be still my heart;
Stirring now
Your sweet, gentle breath
Sweet lei lehua

Chorus
Be true to me, fair one.
Be true to me, I entreat thee.
Give me your hand,
My sweet lei lehua.

My memory of you is always fresh.
I dream of you, my sweet,
At noon and at sunset
My sweet lei lehua.

Victorian Medley:
Flow Gently, Sweet Afton
Gentle Annie

Track 15

Robert Burns
Stephen Foster

Uke 1
Uke 2
F Cm Am Dm
praise; My Ma - ry's a - sleep by thy mur - mur - ing
G7 C F C7 F Dm C7
stream, Flow gen - tly, sweet Af - ton, dis - turb not her

Uke 1
Uke 2
F
1.
F A7
2.
D A7 D
dream. Thou wilt come no more, gen-tle An-nie, Like a
F♯m Bm A7 D A7 Bm
flow'r thy spir-it did de - part; Thou art gone, a - las! like the man-y That have

D A7 D Em G D
Uke 1
bloomed in the sum-mer of my heart. Shall we nev-er more be-hold thee; Nev-er
Uke 2
Bm A7 D Em Bm
Uke 1
hear thy win-ning voice ag - ain When the Spring-time comes gen-tle An-nie, When the
Uke 2

D A7 D A7 D F♯m Em
1.
2.
Uke 1
wild flow'rs are scat - tered o'er the plain?
Uke 2
B dim7 D F♯m A7 D
rit.
Uke 1
Uke 2

Flow Gently, Sweet Afton

Robert Burns

Flow gently, sweet Afton, among thy green braes,
Flow gently, I'll sing thee a song in thy praise;
My Mary's asleep by thy murmuring stream,
Flow gently, sweet Afton, disturb not her dream.

Thou stock-dove, whose echo resounds thro' the glen,
Ye wild whistling blackbirds in yon thorny den,
Thou green-crested lapwing, thy screaming forbear,
I charge you disturb not my slumbering fair.

How lofty, sweet Afton, thy neighboring hills,
Far mark'd with the courses of clear winding rills;
There daily I wander as noon rises high,
My flocks and my Mary's sweet cot in my eye.

How pleasant thy banks and green valleys below,
Where wild in the woodlands the primroses blow;
There oft, as mild Ev'ning sweeps over the lea,
The sweet-scented birk shades my Mary and me.

Thy crystal stream, Afton, how lovely it glides,
And winds by the cot where my Mary resides,
How wanton thy waters her snowy feet lave,
As gathering sweet flowerets she stems thy clear wave.

Gentle Annie

Stephen Foster

Thou wilt come no more, gentle Annie,
Like a flow'r thy spirit did depart;
Thou art gone, alas! like the many
That have bloomed in the summer of my heart.

Shall we never more behold thee;
Never hear thy winning voice again
When the Springtime comes gentle Annie,
When the wild flow'rs are scattered o'er the plain?

We have roamed and loved mid the bowers,
When thy downy cheeks were in their bloom;
Now I stand alone mid the flowers
While they mingle their perfumes o'er thy tomb.

Ah! the hours grow sad while I ponder
Near the silent spot where thou art laid,
And my heart bows down when I wander
By the streams and the meadows where we stray'd.

La Bruja

Track 16

Traditional Mexico

Uke 1
Uke 2
A♭
E♭7
A♭
1.
Fm
2.
B♭m
Fm
C7
B♭m7
C7

18
Uke 1
Uke 2
B♭m6
B♭dim
Fm
Fm
1.
2.
D.C. al Fine

Sentimental Medley

Thomas Moore
Ben Johnson

The Last Rose of Summer

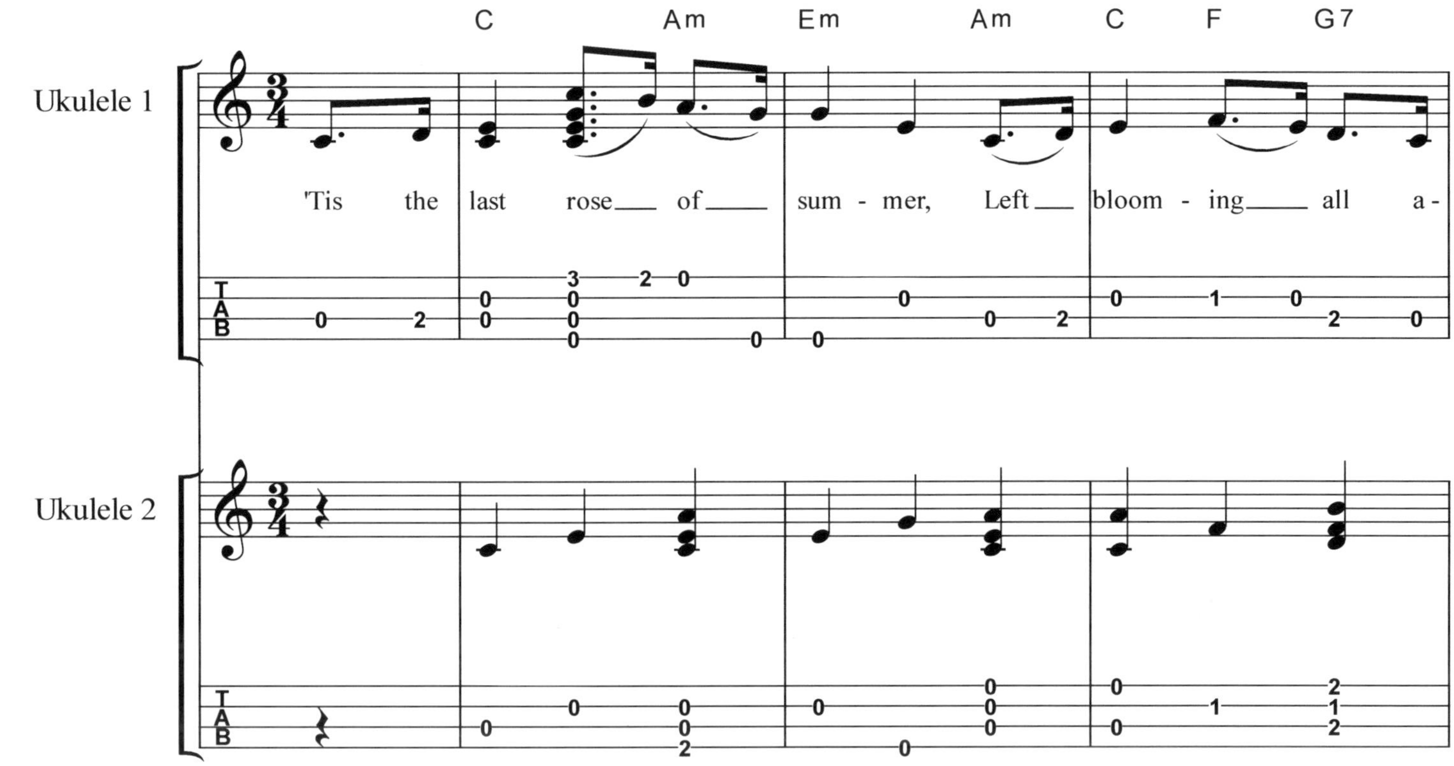

C F Am Em Dm7 Am
Uke 1
gone; No flo - wer of her kin-dred, No rose - bud is
Uke 2
B7 C Am Em Am C F G7
Uke 1
nigh, To re - flect back her blus - hes, Or give sigh for
Uke 2

Drink to Me Only With Thine Eyes

F Bb F C F
Uke 1
I'll not ask for wine. The thirst that from the soul doth rise Doth
Uke 2

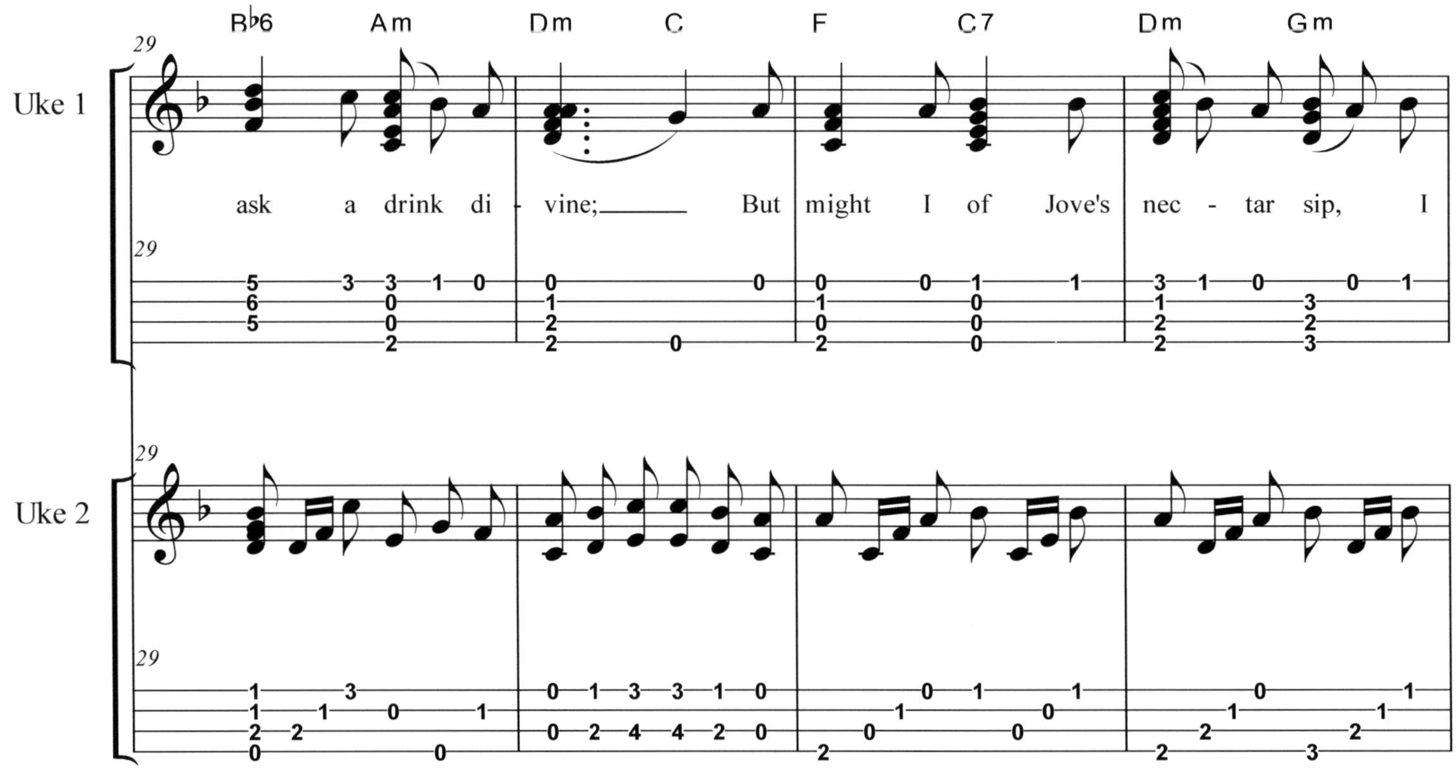
Bb6 Am Dm C F C7 Dm Gm
Uke 1
ask a drink di - vine; But might I of Jove's nec - tar sip, I
Uke 2

Believe Me if All These Endearing Young Charms
Uke 1
Uke 2
F Bb F C F D7 G7 C
would not change for thine.
Be - lieve me, if all those en -
F C Dm C G7 C
dear-ing young charms, Which I gaze on so fond-ly to - day, Were to change by to-mor-row and

F C G7 C
Uke 1
fleet in my arms, Like fair-y gifts fad-ing a - way, Thou wouldst still be a-dored, as this
Uke 2

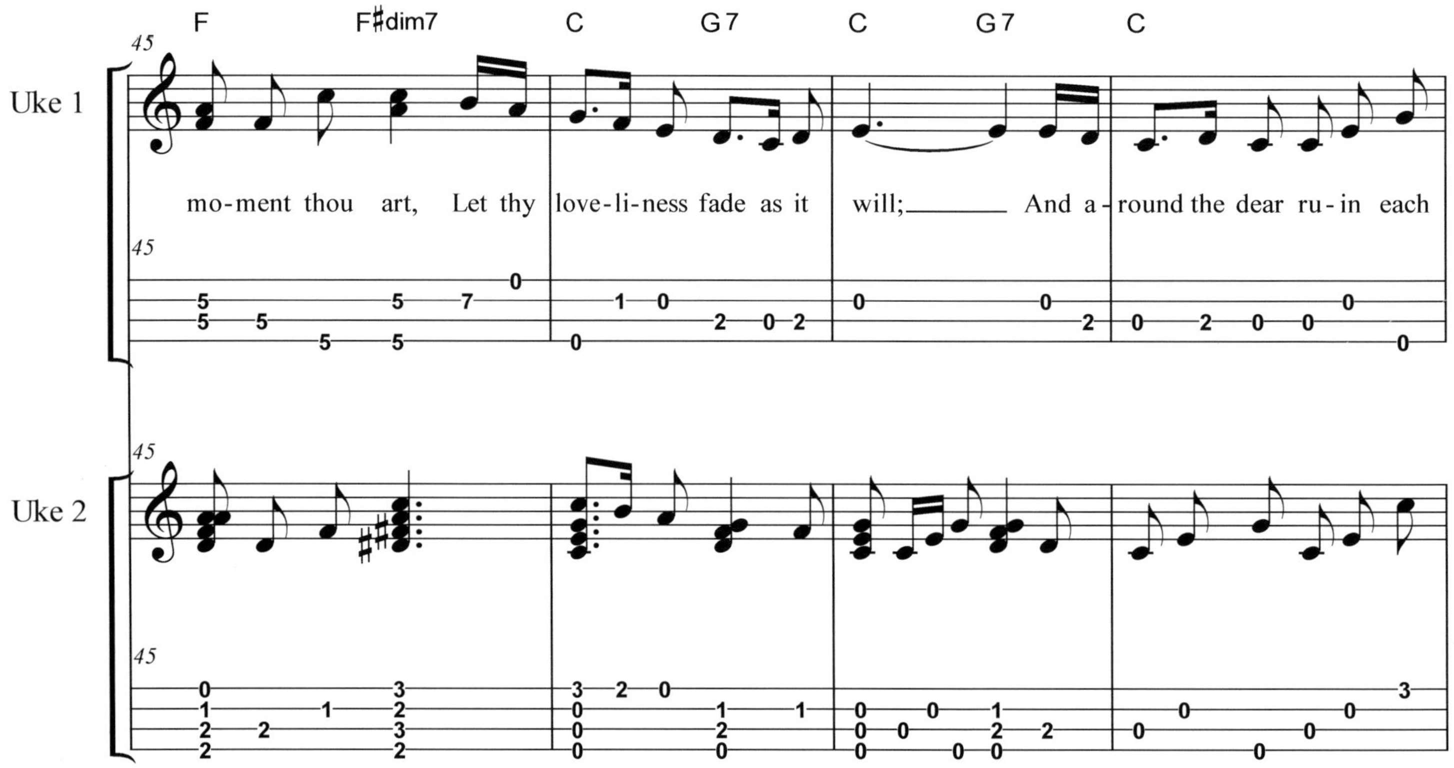
F F♯dim7 C G7 C G7 C
Uke 1
mo-ment thou art, Let thy love-li-ness fade as it will; And a-round the dear ru-in each
Uke 2

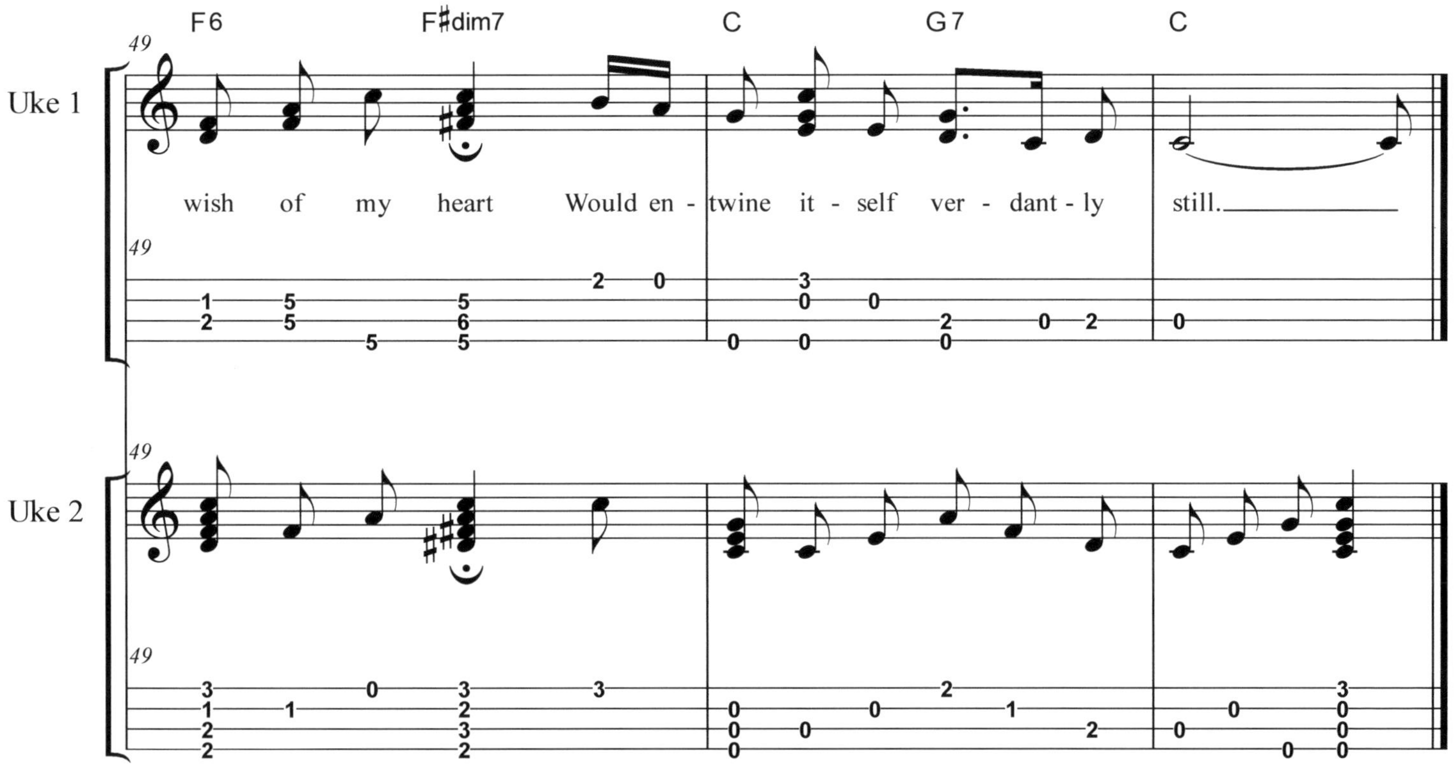

The Last Rose of Summer

Thomas Moore

‘Tis the last rose of summer,
Left blooming all alone;
All her lovely companions
Are faded and gone;
No flower of her kindred,
No rosebud is nigh,
To reflect back her blushes,
Or give sigh for sigh.

I’ll not leave thee, thou lone one!
To pine on the stem;
Since the lovely are sleeping,
Go, sleep thou with them.
Thus kindly I scatter,
Thy leaves o’er the bed,
Where thy mates of the garden
Lie scentless and dead.

So soon may I follow,
When friendships decay,
And from Love’s shining circle
The gems drop away.
When true hearts lie withered,
And fond ones are flown,
Oh! who would inhabit
This bleak world alone?

Drink to Me Only With Thine Eyes

Ben Johnson

Drink to me only with thine eyes,
And I will pledge with mine;
Or leave a kiss within the cup
And I'll not ask for wine.
The thirst that from the soul doth rise
Doth ask a drink divine;
But might I of Jove's nectar sip,
I would not change for thine.

I sent thee late a rosy wreath,
Not so much honouring thee
As giving it a hope that there
It could not withered be;
But thou thereon didst only breathe,
And sent'st it back to me,
Since when it grows and smells, I swear,
Not of itself but thee!

Believe Me, If All Those Endearing Young Charms

Thomas Moore

Believe me, if all those endearing young charms,
Which I gaze on so fondly to-day,
Were to change by to-morrow and fleet in my arms,
Like fairy gifts fading away,
Thou wouldst still be adored, as this moment thou art,
Let thy loveliness fade as it will;
And around the dear ruin each wish of my heart
Would entwine itself verdantly still.

It is not while beauty and youth are thine own,
And thy cheeks unprofaned by a tear,
That the fervor and faith of a soul can be known,
To which time will but make thee more dear.
No, the heart that has truly loved never forgets,
But as truly loves on to the close
As the sunflower turns on her god when he sets
The same look which she turned when he rose.

Gymnopedie #1

Track 18

Eric Satie

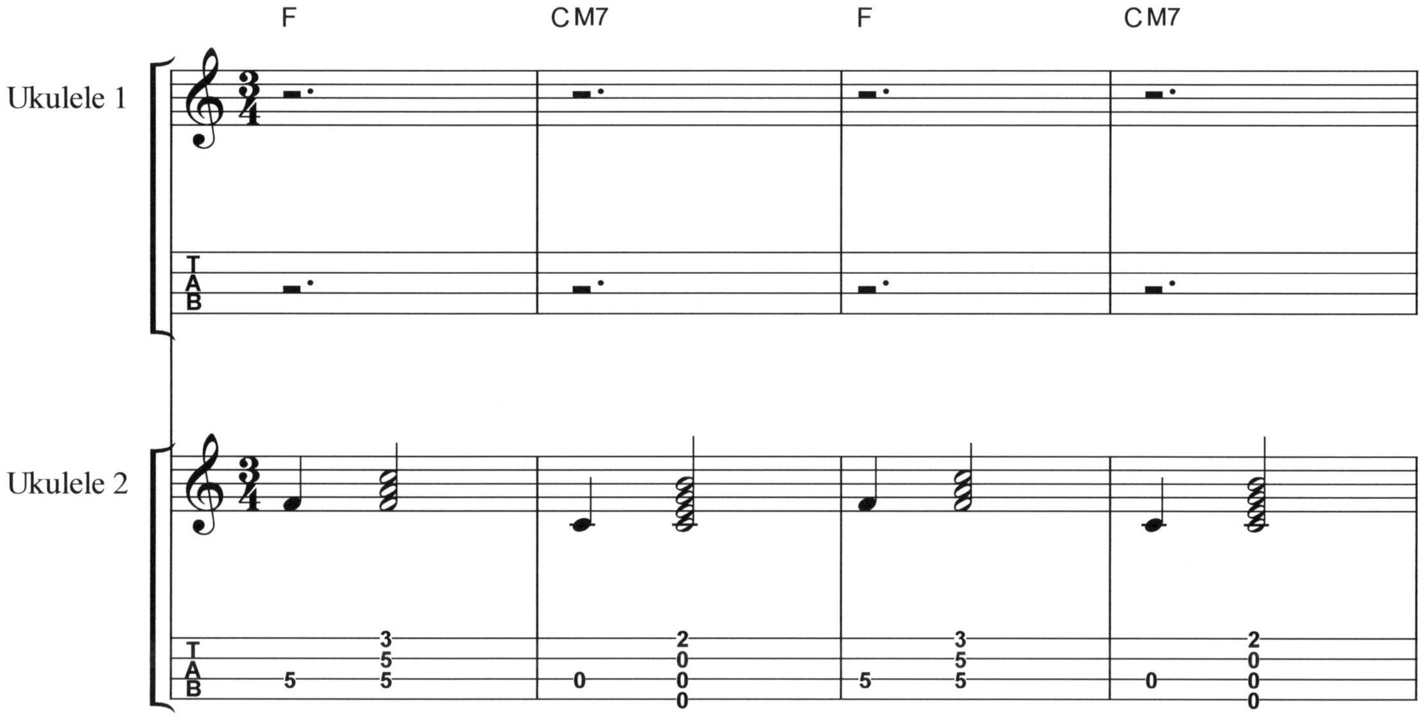

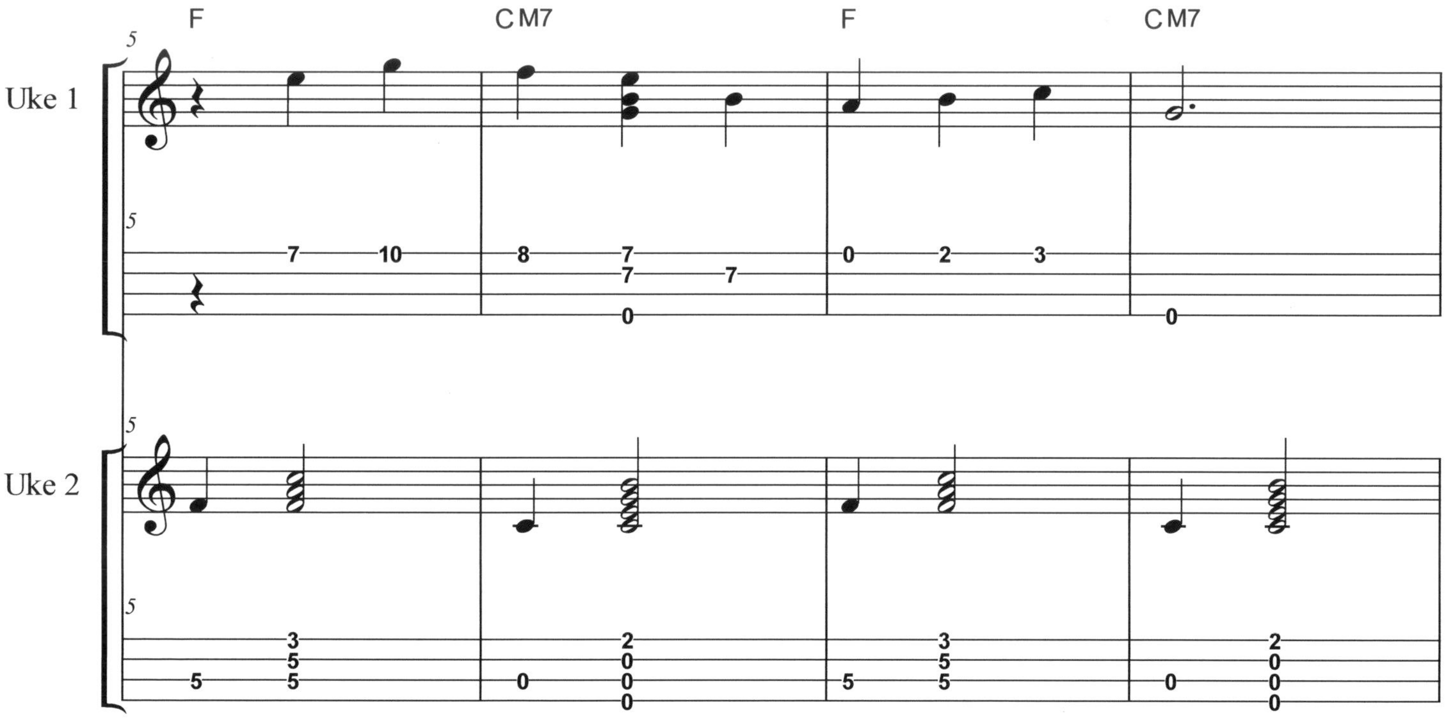

F
CM7
F
CM7
Uke 1
Uke 2
F
CM7
F
CM7
Uke 1
Uke 2

Em
Am7
Dm
Dm7
Uke 1
Uke 2
Cm
Gm
Dm7/C
Uke 1
Uke 2

Uke 1
Uke 2
C7
Gm9
Dsus7#5/C
Dm7/C
C9
Dmin
To Coda 40
Emin
Am7

D.C. al Coda
Bm11/D
CM9/D
A7sus4/D
G min/D
C
E♭M7/D
A7sus4/D
35
Uke 1
Uke 2
Em7(♭5)
Cm9/D
Cm
G min/D
C min
42

About the Songs

Sicilian Waltz
Although I've played this delightful waltz on the mandolin for almost forty years, I have no recollection of where I learned it. I love the way the chords change in the middle of each measure.

Simple Gifts
Composed as a dance by the Shaker elder Joseph Brackett in 1840, "Simple Gifts" is one of America's most widely recognized folksongs. English songwriter Sidney Carter used the melody for his song "Lord of the Dance" in 1963. This duet arrangement expands on the version in "Favorite Old Time American Songs for Ukulele."

The Banks of the Ohio
Beautiful melody, grisly lyrics. Murder ballads are all-too-common in the Anglo-American tradition. This set of lyrics differs slightly from the version in "Favorite Old Time American Songs for Ukulele." I included both this song and "Simple Gifts" to help illustrate how you can take a simple melody and expend it into a complete fingerstyle arrangement.

Margaret's Waltz
When I learned this popular contra dance tune in the1970s, I assumed it was from New England and as old as the hills. Turns out it was written in 1959 by an Englishman, Pat Shaw. It's given here in the usual fiddle key of A major.

Ahi Wela (Fire of Love)
Written in 1881 by Lizzy Doirin and Mary Beckley, close friends of Hawaii's Royal Family. While often danced by little children, the lyrics describe love's passion in no uncertain terms. Oddly, the melody may be Russian.

The Cuckoo Round
This three-part round appears under several different names, both as an instrumental or with lyrics in French or English. It's even better with three ukes.

The Skye Boat Song
Charles Edward Stuart, the "Lad Born to be King," fled Scotland following the disastrous battle of Culloden Moor on April 16, 1746. The sparse pentatonic melody conveys a palpable sense of longing.

Ua Like No a Like
Alice Everett, one of a circle of skilled composers that included Queen Liliuokalani, published this lovely song in 1912. It is also known with English words under the title "Constancy."

Scarborough Fair
This English folksong with its haunting Dorian mode melody first came to the world's attention in the 1960s. Like many such riddle songs, a lover is asked to perform impossible feats to prove that her love is true.

'Akaka Falls
The waterfall on the Big Island of Hawaii is the scene of a romantic story involving a suicide and not one, but two, grieving lovers. Helen Parker wrote lyrics to this traditional melody in the 1930s. This instrumental arrangement is based on one Keola Beamer and I created for our Mel Bay book "Learn to Play Hawaiian Slack Key Guitar."

Hard Times, Come Again No More
Stephen Foster's stunning prayer of compassion was composed in 1854. First recorded on a wax cylinder in 1915, in more recent times the song has been a staple of Bluegrass and Americana singers.

Fandanguillo
I found an undated, anonymous guitar score for this etude at the back of my file cabinet. My uke arrangement more or less divides the bass and treble parts between the two ukes. The title – a diminutive of fandango – refers to both a type of dance and a party featuring dancing and music.

Home Sweet Home
Everyone has heard this song, but few know its curious history. The original poem was written by John Howard Payne, an American expatriot, for the 1823 Italian opera "Clari." Soon after, Sir Henry Bishop, an Englishman, set the words to

music–possibly using a Sicilian melody. Few today know the original lyrics or melody, but at one time it was the most popular song in the world!

Sweet Lei Lehua
A beautiful example of the songwriting skills of Hawaii's royal family. King David Kalākaua's "Sweet Lei Lehua" was published in "Kings Hawaiian Melodies" in 1916. Royal Hawaiian Band leader Henry Berger is sometimes credited with the lilting melody. This challenging arrangement utilizes some of the twists and turns typical of Hawaiian slack key guitar.

Victorian Medley
During the Victorian era, well bred young men and women whiled away the hours playing "parlor music" like these tender songs on the guitar or piano. This is what it might have sounded like had they known about the ukulele.

Flow Gently Sweet Afton
The Scottish poet Robert Burns wrote the "Afton Water" in 1791. It is possibly a lament for his beloved "Highland Mary" Campbell. The poem was set to music in 1837 by Kentuckian Jonathan Spillman while he was in law school.

Gentle Annie
Stephen Foster's exquisite song of loss and yearning was written in 1856 and set to a traditional Irish melody. Although Foster was no stranger to bereavement, we do not know who the song commemorates.

La Bruja
"La Bruja" (The Sorceress) is a Mexican folk song from Veracruz. This version comes from a yellowed manuscript I dug out of my files, written in a hand I do not recognize. As with all folk songs, numerous variations of the melody and lyrics may be found.

Sentimental Medley
Three favorite poems of love undying that have stood the test of time.

The Last Rose of Summer
Dublin born Thomas Moore (1779-1852) is often called "the Irish Robert Burns." His ballads – including "The Harp That Once Through Tara's Halls" and "The Minstrel Boy" – were published in "Moore's Irish Melodies" in 1846. "The Last Rose of Summer," written in 1805, was published in song form with this melody ten years later. Moore's music was hugely popular in his time but has faded from view recently.

Drink to Me Only With Thine Eyes
Ben Johnson's 1616 poem, "Song. To Celia," fits this sweet melody like a glove. But no one is sure exactly where the music comes from, or even if Johnson had anything to do with setting his poem to the tune. I first learned it from a dulcimer player in Virginia; proof that a beautiful song has no boundaries.

Believe Me if All these Endearing Young Charms
Thomas Moore wrote these poignant lyrics to a traditional Irish air in 1808. The song was written for his wife, who had become a recluse over her fears of being seen with the scars of smallpox. The melody is also used for the alma mater of Harvard University.

Gymnopedie #1
One of three piano pieces published in 1888 by the eccentric French composer Eric Satie. Satie was worlds ahead of his time–his music presaged minimalism, ambient music, and even industrial and techno: the score for his ballet "Parade" includes typewriters, foghorns and milk bottles! The three Gymnopedies are perhaps Satie's best known works.

I based this arrangement on several sources, including a piano score and a handful of solo guitar arrangements. Satie's use of dissonance was profound; in wrangling some of the huge chords onto the limited range of two ukuleles I was forced to make some interesting harmonic choices. Nor can I vouch for all of the chord names; these represent my best guesses. I take full responsibility for any musical harm this may cause.

No one can say precisely what the title means, by the way. Satie liked it that way.

Mark Kailana Nelson

Multi-instrumentalist Mark Nelson has carved a unique niche for himself as an entertainer, musician and educator. His deep love and understanding of traditional music led him to the mastery of several different musical idioms, ranging from blues to old time music, Celtic to Hawaiian. In a career that began well before he was able to drive, he has performed everywhere from street corners and hay barns to festivals and the concert stage in the US, Europe and Canada. He once worked as a banjo playing gorilla in Dublin, but that's a different story.

Mark lives in Southern Oregon's Applegate Valley with his wife Annie and various furred friends, where he divides his time between studio work, writing, and watching the trees grow.

Selected Discography

Juke'n The Uke: Blues, Ragtime & Hokum for 'Ukulele
Slack Key Style 'Ukulele
Funtime Uke-A-Rama
Ke Kukima Polinahe
Old Time Hawaiian Slack Key Guitar
The Water is Wide
autumn…
The Faery Hills
After the Morning
The Rights of Man

Books

Mastering Ukulele Chord Inversions (Mel Bay Publications)
Favorite Old Time American Songs for Ukulele (Mel Bay Publications)
Favorite Fingerstyle Solos for Ukulele (Mel Bay Publications)
Learn to Play Fingerstyle Solos for Ukulele (Mel Bay Publications)
Learn to Play Hawaiian Slack Key Guitar (Mel Bay Publications)
Favorite Old Time American Songs for Appalachian Dulcimer (Mel Bay Publications)
The Complete Collection of Celtic Music for Appalachian Dulcimer (Mel Bay Publications)

Juke'n The Uke: Blues, Ragtime & Hokum for 'Ukulele (acme arts)
Learn to Play Slack Key Style Ukulele (acme arts)
Old Time Hawaiian Slack Key Guitar (acme arts)
Ke Kukima Polinahe: Hawaiian Music For Dulcimer (acme arts)
Fiddle Tunes for Dulcimer: The Rights of Man (acme arts)

Mark Nelson • Acme Arts
PO Box 967 • Jacksonville, OR 97530
www.Mark-o.com

Be sure to check out Mark's ever-expanding series of free on-line video lessons.

Notes

WWW.MELBAY.COM